CARING FOR MOM

CARING FOR MOM

Midlife Reflections

Dorothy Sander

ISBN 978-0-557-32423-1
Copyright 2010 By Dorothy J. Sander
Printed in the United States of America

Cover photo and design by Dorothy Sander

Aging Abundantly Press
Durham, NC

FOREWARD

This book contains a selection of blogs written over a period of two years for Women Etcetera! as well as articles and journal entries written during the same time frame. Women Etceterea! is an organization by and for women over fifty (read more page on page 117).

The women I have met through Women Etcetera! have inspired and encouraged me and each other since its inception. My life has been forever changed as a result and without them this book would not have been possible.

My love and appreciation go most especially to Suzanne Caplan, who is and has been the driving force behind WE. She carries the torch, pushing and prodding every step of the way to create a place where women of wisdom can come together to explore their gifts and make the most of who they are.

My love and gratitude go also to Jill and Celia, who know my heart and soul and love me anyway. Thank you for your continued support and encouragement as together we struggle to make sense of life.

My deepest love and appreciation goes without saying to my life companion, my consistent and constant champion and the love of my life. He has never wavered in his support and belief in me. He is my rock, my joy, my hope and has had the strength and determination to hold my hand as I walked down each painful and difficult road I have faced. Without him I would have neither faith in myself or God. I owe him my life.

Dorothy Sander, January 2010

For Scott

and our sons Jeremy and Devon
who mean everything to me.

In Memory of
Frances Anne Wickersham Hoffman
1911 - 2008

CONTENTS

MIDLIFE TRANSITIONS

No matter how old we are or what our life circumstances, life altering events happen, sometimes frequently. They are the situations, real or imagined, that drive us to our knees. They may be as clearly defined as the death of a spouse or a painful divorce or as subtle as restlessness in our chosen career.

A life crisis can be brought on by external or internal events, but either way, it gives us an opportunity to grow and to create lives that are far richer than they were before. Every time we face a crisis of any proportion, we have a choice. We can allow it to debilitate us or we can use it to foster and support change and personal growth.

Coming through a crisis requires navigating the treacherous waters of emotional, mental and physical upheaval. We must stare down our demons and step into the fire of change, allowing it to burn away the useless debris that may have put a stranglehold on our lives. When we do this, we come forth, in the end, with a reconstructed self that more perfectly matches the person we were meant to be. We are then able to see and use our trials and tribulations, not as a force of destruction but to forge new strength, develop more clarity, and to define our vision more precisely. We may then more easily resolve to live our dreams with greater intent and purpose. The process informs us. If we dare to listen, it teaches us things we need to know about ourselves. It opens doors to the very things we have yearned to discover to enable us to live more authentic lives.

Transition is a process that contains stages that are very similar to those outlined by Elizabeth Kubler Ross in her famous book "On Death and Dying". Accepting transition as a process helps us understand that while life altering events are painful, they also contain the exact ingredients we need to garner a deeper understanding of ourselves and our lives. We do not need to live "lives of quiet desperation". We can step into the fire of change and be made new.

Too often we look at our problems as forces beyond our control. We think that our only option is to try to absorb these events and survive, or to fight back with anger and rage. As a result we get stuck in the muck of emotional conflagration and end up going back and forth, back and forth, unable to come through to the other side. When we resist change, it slows the process and prevents our healing and growth.

It is human nature to avoid pain and to seek comfort. Erich Fromm wrote, "Every act of birth requires the courage to let go of something, to let go of the breast, to let go of the lap, to let go of the hand, to let go eventually of all certainties, and to rely only upon one thing: one's own power to be aware and to respond; that is, one's own creativity." This is the essence of transition.

Caring for an aging parent is a life crisis that can stymie us and wear us down or it can lead us into a period of transition that will teach us about ourselves. Midlife gives us plenty of opportunity for growth and is fertile ground for resolving past issues and stepping into the future stronger and more grounded than ever before.

The reflections in this book were written during just such a time in my life. While it was a very painful and stressful process, it led me to take steps I would not otherwise have taken. I have learned the value of walking through the fire, allowing it to burn away a lifetime of debris and step out into the light just a little bit smarter and a little bit lighter.

My hope is that as you read these reflections, you will feel less alone when facing your own trials and catch a glimpse of the value inherent in the pain and difficulty of all midlife transitions.

TURNING FIFTY

Though it has been a few years since I turned fifty I still use it as some sort of benchmark. Something happened in my life around that time. A deep, tremulous eruption began to stir both within and without. The ground, quite unexpectedly, began to shift beneath my feet.

On the surface I can point to empty nest, menopause and caring for an aging parent as the perfect storm that created the impetus for change. But on the inside, it was as if everything I had refused to face about myself decided to say, "Okay, enough. It's time to change. It's time to live the life you were meant to live."

Life decided to hand me one crisis after another until I could no longer hold on to my preconceived notions about whom and what I was or should be. Through this period of time one of the more stressful and heart wrenching experiences I faced was the death of my parents.

It's difficult to grasp the full spectrum of ways in which our parents shaped us until they are gone. A perceptual shift takes place that is impossible to anticipate. In some visceral way their shadow evaporates. It's not that the many annoying habits of thought we learned from them are suddenly gone, because they are not, it's simply that our perspective changes. They have less power over us and we can see both them and ourselves more clearly. But, in order to do this we must first grieve the loss.

Even before we reach this point, many of us are faced with the whole process of caring for our parents in their decline precisely at a time when our resources are already stretched thin. Chances are we have children who are entering adulthood and dealing with the terror that erupts in the heart of most parents at this time. We may also be at the pinnacle of our careers or becoming painfully aware that we've missed the mark. As women, we are going through menopause and not only dealing with hormonal fluctuations but struggling with the physical and emotional upheaval that goes along with it. We are questioning what it means to be a woman, a wife, and a female as our bodies begin to show signs of aging.

We can't choose the timing of menopause or death, so we simply hang on and ride out the waves of destruction until, with God's grace, we somehow get to shore.

In the process, the fire of change can help us forge a new life. If we are lucky we don't give in to the devastation but use it as an opportunity to make positive changes.

THE FANTASY OF YOUTH

Lately I have been reflecting on the lost optimism of my youth, once such an integral part of who I was. Its absence disturbs me. I want it back! I want to feel all that giddy hope and excitement about the future I once had, the deep conviction that any problem could be solved, any dream could come true. I don't like what has replaced this feeling; the relentless fear and anxiety that insist a catastrophe is just waiting around the corner.

When I was young, I was convinced I could and *would* have it all. Even in the middle of a clinical depression, I believed the future held hope. I walked forward knowing, not just believing, that one day my dreams would come true, or at least some acceptable version of them.

Somewhere along the way that joie de vivre went up in smoke. I'm waiting for it to be replaced with something deeper...like peace and wisdom.

The shift from hope to fear took place somewhere around the time I turned fifty. My husband had a heart attack and I came to the sudden and terrifying realization that he was not invincible, and neither was I. Our future together was anything but secure, regardless of our undying love for one another. In addition, career and life choices hadn't worked out the way I had expected them to and to make matters worse I became acutely aware that I was running out of time.

Prior to the moment when the shift took place, I had been so focused on the daily struggles of raising children and making ends meet that I hadn't noticed the time slipping by.

Years of relentless stress has taken its toll on my resilience and willingness to try new paths. I'm beginning to feel the aging process reshaping my sense of who I am. I don't like what I'm seeing and I desperately want a do-over.

We all hear stories about how "it's never too late" to start something new. It doesn't matter how old we are. Look at Colonel Sanders! He was seventy when he started Kentucky Fried Chicken. But he had something I don't seem to have! Hope!

Without the optimism and sense of timelessness that is a given when we are young, it's not so easy to take careless risks and damn the consequences. To sit idly by and watch the days go by, terrified to make a change doesn't seem a welcome option either.

I can't help but wonder how I am supposed to live with the uncertainty and complexity that has woven its way into my psyche. I used to be a person of faith but even that has been eroded by the ridiculousness of modern day religion and the inadequacies of the traditional ones.

This may sound like a diatribe of pure and utter hopelessness. You're probably asking yourself, "is she depressed?" "Order the Prozac!" But I think it's something quite different. I believe it's a change many of us go through at some point midway through our lives. We begin asking ourselves some hard questions, like how do we find hope in the face of certain death? Where can we discover joy when it hurts to get up in the morning or when we are plagued by illness? How can we look for newness in a life that has beaten us up and robbed us of our hope and faith?

I don't have the answers just yet. I do know, however, that I am not ready to give up on finding something of value to replace the lost, and sorely missed, optimism of youth.

REFLECTIONS FROM THE MIDDLE

I am sitting beside my mother, now in her nineties, taking in the early summer colors from my porch. The Day Lilies still color the landscape as the Cone Flowers begin to make their statement. Mom is here for one of her increasingly frequent visits. "I need to get away from the inmates," she tells me and I know it's time for me to drive the two hours to retrieve her from the retirement community. She lives alone now, since my father's death two years ago. She is not happy living the community lifestyle after a lifetime of having her own home and family always nearby.

It's a quiet weekday morning. The birds are in full song. I've escaped from my office for a moment and the nature reminds me to stop a moment and breathe, to take in the fresh air and quiet. I find it increasingly difficult to relax. The stress of running a home business, two teenage sons, two dogs, a cat, a husband/business partner, a multitude of chores and the increasing stress and frustration of the electronic age is taking its toll.

"I have never seen Hydrangeas like that before", Mom says as she points in the direction of my prized shrub. It is one of my favorites as well but I can't help but mentally roll my eyes at her comment.

Of course she's "seen Hydrangeas like that"! She saw this very one last year and she's lived in the South for more than twenty years. I silently chastise myself for being impatient with her forgetfulness.

Whether its forgetfulness or a renewed appreciation for life in the face of its nearing end, she seems to look at things differently these days.

"Hmmm," I say instead of what I'm thinking. My eyes stray to one of my many ill-arranged gardens. I ponder what plant to put where to achieve some artistic balance. Before I decide, I skip ahead, mentally trimming an azalea. I feel restless. Mom continues to gaze upon the Hydrangea. I envy her patience.

Our friendly Carolina Wren lands on the bird feeder and brings my attention back to the porch with his boisterous yet ill-fitting song.

"I love the Carolina Wren," I say, trying to speak softly so as not to scare it away.

"Yes, I do too," Mom replies. She maintains her almost century old practice of absolute stillness, as she does whenever a bird is near. It's as if she isn't breathing.

The summer I was ten, she took me with her on one of her early morning "bird walks." I followed along sleepily. I was bored and miserable. She walked quietly, occasionally pointing out ferns and wildflowers when she was certain her voice would not frighten a bird away. She recited the name of each one.

Now, she struggles to remember *our* names and I remind her that the fern in my garden is a "Cinnamon Fern." She's in remarkable health for her age. All of five feet tall and a hundred pounds, she's a bit unsteady, but manages to do all my ironing, wash the dishes and put fresh flowers on the table every day during her visit. She reminds me of the importance of the little things in life. This visit she re-planted my many hanging baskets, carefully watering them daily *and* sweeping off both of our decks. Left to me, the baskets would remain unkempt another season and definitely un-watered!

"What did you do for fun when you were a teenager, Mom?" I ask.

"What did I do? Well, we moved around so much...."

"What were your days like when you were sixteen?" I ask because I've begun to worry about my boys and the affect technology seems to be having on them. They seem so stressed and I read that teens are experiencing burnout, and there is a higher incidence of teen suicide, teen homicide, and drug abuse. Things must have been simpler in mother's youth. I'm looking for a clue.

"I was in the orchestra. We traveled around the state giving concerts. It was quite an adventure." How different from the trips to Europe and amusement parks many high school students now take.

Music, like birds and plants, is one of my mother's passions. Thankfully, she passed it on to me. My parents took me to Lincoln Center to hear the New York Philharmonic and to the Metropolitan Opera to watch

Madame Butterfly. We also took in musicals and plays whenever we could.

Like the bird walks, I hated being pulled away from my little social world, but trapped in the concert hall, I had little choice but to listen. What I didn't learn to appreciate by choice, I learned to love in time.

I think of my sixteen year old son upstairs on his computer and wish he had experienced some of the things I did. My husband and I joyfully share our love of classic rock with our children, laughing together at how unlike our parents we are. I'm quietly proud when my son tells me, "You were so lucky to grow up with all that great music!" He views our trip to Woodstock as a trip to Nirvana.

"So, Mom, what else did you do when you were sixteen?" I continue.

"I lived in the country and I didn't have many friends, so I did a lot of this," she says as her arm creates a brush stroke across the yard. "I built ponds and bird baths out of stone and cement. I showed you a picture, didn't I?" She had, several times.

"We had dinner parties at school because we weren't allowed to dance - the religious beliefs of the people in the area prevented dancing. But, we all dressed up, had a dinner and managed to enjoy ourselves.

My oldest son's recent Senior Prom was not nearly so simple. Dressed in a $150 rented tuxedo, his date wearing a dress that cost at least that much, the couple was picked up by a limousine and driven to the best restaurant in town before attending the Prom. This was done not because we're wealthy, but because it is just what is done! My Prom, thirty four years ago, was more like my son's than my mothers, but we drove our parent's car and my mother made my prom dress, spending about $15 on fabric.

"I liked to read," she continued, interrupting my thoughts.

"Where did you shop?" I ask.

"Shop? We didn't shop. What did we need to shop for?"

"Well, food for one thing. And clothes."

"There was a grocery store in town. My mother would call them up, read a list off and they'd deliver it. Free of charge, of course."

"What about clothes?"

"I made over many of my aunt's cast offs. I suppose on occasion we'd go to the city nearby for a few things."

"It must have been very quiet then," I reflect as I hear a car go up the road and a plane fly overhead. Images of the shopping mall, Best Buy, Wal-Mart and, good Lord deliver me, Abercrombie & Fitch float through my mind. I cringe at the thought of the nerve shattering music and sense-overloading piles of merchandise. Shopping is a nightmare of never-ending choices. "Will you take me to Best Buy?" has been my son's mantra since it opened six years ago.

At fifty three, knee deep in the consumer, electronic age, I'm ready to go back to the simpler times of my mother's youth.

"I guess it was difficult at times," she continued as if reading my mind. We had to do without many things because of the war. Like sugar. We'd get a few cups every two or three months."

Cups? Imagine living without sugar! I recently read that Americans consume two thirds cup of sugar a day, an interesting contrast to one third cup a month. As a child we never drank soda and only had dessert on special occasions.

The phone rings, interrupting our walk down memory lane. "Did you have phones back then?" I sigh as I get up to answer it.

Stepping back into the house, the quiet vanishes. The hum of the office computer, the whoosh of the air conditioner, the thump and crash of a video game, a dog rushing eagerly to greet me, my cell phone ringing two seconds behind the house phone...

I watch out the window as I field a telemarketer, looking for the calming presence of the Carolina Wren and the soothing image of my mother sitting peacefully...and very, very still.

AWAKE!

Often these days when I press my ear to the ground I hear a hum of discontent. People everywhere are struggling with the pressures and stress of modern society. We are interrupted constantly by our cell phones, the call of email and Internet, televisions in restaurants, advertisers in our face, pressuring us and telling us what we should have, what we should buy and what we should do. It feels akin to an electric cattle prod to the soul.

It has become more important for today's fifty plus woman to stand back from these pressures. We are a fortunate group of people as we still have a vague memory of what it was like before technology. Our children and their children will never know the calm before the storm.

We still remember the quiet of a household before the infestation of computers, cell phones and numerous flat-panel, wide screen TVs. One TV per household was thought to be sufficient. Thirty second commercials only occurred once or twice each thirty minutes. There was never time to get a snack! Now we can get a snack, do a load of laundry and wash the dishes without missing our show.

New movies only came out a couple of times a year and stayed in the local theater for weeks and sometimes months. Everything moved slower then. Have you watched an old movie or television show from the 1950's lately? I know you fell asleep. So did I. We've been changed.

It's time to remind ourselves to reflect and remember the quiet moments that used to be and to acknowledge their value. Quiet is the door to our soul. Perhaps that is why God appears to be silent. We can't hear Him anymore over the roar of our world. Quiet intensifies the senses. In silence we see more...feel more...smell and taste more acutely. Eating by candlelight is a very different experience from eating in a fast food restaurant.

Taking time each day to shut off the noise and listen to the quiet may help us re-awaken our senses. Each one offers us a different perspective on life. The smell of a rose may evoke memories of our grandmother's garden. The lilt of Enya may quicken our spirit. The perfect beauty of a sunset may restore our faith in God.

Take time to really see the beauty of nature around you, the fresh new foliage as spring unfolds, the colorful vibrant flowers of summer, the brilliant oranges and reds of the leaves as they turn in the fall. Take it in. Really see it. Smell the aroma of freshly cut grass, the damp earth, lilac trees and hyacinths. Awaken your sense of taste with the juices of a fresh orange, the crunch of a handful of salted nuts. Notice these things again.

As the seasons change so shall you. Discover what lessons are to be learned by watching and taking in the death and rebirth of nature. In so doing, you may not only awaken your spirit but perhaps just touch the hand of God.

WHERE HAVE ALL THE FLOWERS GONE

In the late 1960's, when I was in my youth, we railed against materialism, both the mindset that created it and the soul numbing results it left behind. Our generation was determined to *be* different - to make a difference - to forgo luxury for the betterment of society.

A couple of years ago I awoke from the hyper focused years of child rearing to discover that my generation had sold out! We reared our children, not with a sense of values, but in abject indulgence! Were we lying to ourselves in the sixties or didn't we realize how difficult it would be to live out our convictions. If the truth is told, at nineteen we were probably just enamored with the notion of peace, love and rock and roll! What nineteen-year-old isn't intoxicated with a sense of his/her own power? I would like to believe we were not that shallow.

I bucked societal trends and chose to stay at home with my children. The whole time I felt like a failure as I watched my friends and peers "doing it all". I comforted myself with the conviction that my children would be happier, better adjusted adults because they were not relegated to a life of day care and nannies. I was determined that they would have their Mom and Dad and dinner time together every day of the week. My young adult offspring have not *yet* displayed this esoteric effect to the degree I expected. My friends who chose the career route have well adjusted children too. In fact, the majority of my children's peers have not been raised in a two parent household. Will this difference create its own set of problems when it comes time for them to marry and choose a spouse? They are good, responsible, kind people who value the family connection. Perhaps this is enough.

Many of the members of my generation of peace, love and hippie beads chose to climb the corporate ladder and do nothing about healthcare or free-flowing illegal immigration. We can blame the government all we want for these problems but *we* are to blame. We elected the leaders. We refused to speak loudly enough about our dissatisfaction to make change happen the way we thought we would. We became the "me generation".

Now at mid-life, I find I am in a very different place from where I thought I would be and I'm pretty sure I'm not the only one. It's time to start a new revolution...to ferret out the lost hippies of yesteryear and reignite the flame to put meaning back into our lives. It's time to recapture the lost optimism of our youth, add the wisdom we have earned and begin to make a difference. Now. There are fewer tomorrows for us. It's time to back to the core values we left at Woodstock and make the world a better place. Care to join me?

THE DANGER ZONE

I sat at my desk the other day, staring out of the window at our barren maple tree, the cold of winter leaving it barren. It looked dignified and beautiful in its nakedness. I searched its form for some life altering thought to spark my writing.

I was brought back to reality by an odd and persistent smell. I sniffed the air trying to figure out what the odor might be, even as I hoped it would go away and leave me in peace to write.

Was it animal or human? Something my husband was cooking, perhaps? Maybe it was just my imagination. I turned my attention back to the tree and the cars going down the road.

My husband had just left to run errands and I held a glorious hour of peace and quiet precariously in my hands. There has been little of it lately, with the kids home from college and the winter months keeping Scott at home busily cooking and cleaning in a desperate attempt to burn off the nervous energy of the slow season.

I clung to my keyboard even as the aroma grew stronger with each passing moment. It would not be denied. Annoyed, I grabbed my coffee cup (if I had to evacuate I was not leaving *it* behind!) and set off to track down the offender, deal with it and get back to work ASAP.

As I approached the kitchen the smell grew stronger. It was not the smell of a pot left on the stove or burning food. I know *those* smells intimately!

In an instant my eyes began to burn. The kitchen was filled with smoke. I buried my nose in the crook of my arm and waved my free hand in a frantic attempt to part the seas of smoke to see what was causing it.

There, lying on our glass top stove was a smoldering dishtowel, just seconds away from erupting into flames. I grabbed a corner and flung it into the sink, dousing it with a blast of water from the faucet. Those damn flat stoves are a fire hazard! And so is my husband!

The two of us, though quite different, have always had one thing in common. We both need a "danger zone" sign hung around our necks. It was one thing when we were younger but now as we get older it's getting worse and we're not even "old" yet!

I think the time is nearing to hire live in counter measures or install two smoke detectors in every room -- Oh, Lord! Come to think of it, the smoke detector did not even go off! We probably haven't tested them in years. Good grief. We're doomed.

SPRING

Spring is my favorite time of year. The birds announce new versions of old songs and the dull gray landscape dons a cloak in shades of virgin green. In the springtime I am reminded that there is goodness in life even in the worst of circumstances.

When we are shivering and struggling through the cold months preceding spring, it is hard to imagine that anything exists that can supply the warmth and sustenance we crave. It is much the same in life. When discouragement mounts and ice forms on our world, the future can look bleak. Days remain frozen by mass disappointment and we struggle to see the hope the future holds. Sometimes, if we draw a blanket around our shoulders and hunker down before a fire, we can stoke the flames within us to keep us warm as we await an early thaw.

When we are trapped in our struggles it is easy to become so focused on our discomfort that we cannot see the spark of hope that is may be right in front of us. We feel stuck and as the cold bears down upon us we panic, flailing our arms, trying to break free. Being trapped in a winter period of our life can seem endless and terrifying.

It may, however, be precisely where we need to be... within ourselves...until we find the inner strength to take the next step. It is there we will find the courage to shuck off the blanket of fear and pain and allow the first rays of the warming spring sun to shine on us from just beyond the trees.

If a recent dark, stormy period of your life continues to fray your edges, don't be afraid to turn inward for a time, to pull back from the ravages of the frozen tundra and keep yourself warm, by believing that the end is in sight. Because it is.

Hold tight to the promises of spring -- of rebirth -- of knowing we are all part of the same creation that produces the buds outside of your window each and every year.

Time heals. And, just as a tree finds the life-force to bloom each Spring, we too can we survive a winter season in our lives, knowing we will, in time, once again feel the warmth of the sun upon our face.

SHARING THE JOURNEY

I used to look forward to calling my mother each weekend, to fill her in on the goings-on in my life and catch up on the latest family gossip. She is the focal point of our family, keeping us abreast of each other's activities. Her five children don't take the time to call each another, probably because we all talk to Mom.

In the last few months I've come to dread these phone calls. Now ninety six, Mom doesn't remember what I tell her from one call to the next. She struggles to carry on a conversation and I struggle to hold up both sides of it. I miss the conversations we used to have.

She has been a part of my life since the day I was born and knows things about me I don't know about myself. I've travelled through so much of life by myself now, and much of it I chose not to share with her. But, I always knew she was there if I needed her.

She loves my husband, and my children like only a grandparent can. Does she drive me crazy? Of course. And yet I can't imagine not having her in my life. Every time I pick up the phone to call her, I hope that she will be the way she used to be.

We have reversed positions. I am now her caretaker. She needs me, and just as she was always there for me, I will be there for her. She's alone now, frail and afraid, and often filled with sadness as she learns of the death of one more friend or family member. And yet, in so many ways, she is filled with joy for all she has experienced. I want to walk her last mile with her, loving and supporting her as I am able, even if she no longer knows I'm there.

I find it impossible to imagine her in an institution being cared for by strangers. It seems a travesty that children of aging parents should allow themselves to become so busy and caught up in their day to day lives that they can't take the time to be present for their parents through the last years of their lives. It isn't easy and I don't always want to do it, but in my heart of hearts it is what I know I must do, for myself as much as for her.

There seems to be a trend in our society to hand off family responsibilities to others, from child care to caring for our elderly parents. We have become self-centered and preoccupied with our own agendas and in the process we are missing out on an opportunity to grow and experience the richness of life. It does include pain and hardship, but I believe I am richer for the time I have spent with her these last few years. We haven't always seen eye-to-eye and childhood hurts still linger. But she is my mother. I owe her something. I owe myself something.

MAKING CHOICES

Life demands so much from each of us. Whether we are doing what we love or are buried in circumstances we hate, we still have to face each day, look fear and uncertainty in the eye, and move forward. Our path is seldom clear, even if we have an inkling of direction. The water is just murky enough to give us pause.

It doesn't matter if we are a person who forges ahead with gusto or one who plods along agonizing over each step. The course is the same. We must make choices every day; simple, complex, insignificant, monumental choices, each piling up, one upon the other. Answered or unanswered these choices are the building blocks of our lives both creating what it has been, what it is and what it will be.

Most of the time there are no obvious right or wrong choices, just shades of gray that we squint anxiously to discern. Perhaps if we chose to give up squinting to "see" the answer, and quietly closed our eyes instead, we might hear the voice of our hearts, where all true answers lie. A quiet voice exists within each us and it knows the answers. It speaks more often in nuances than bold statements and requires us to be utterly still to hear, but it is there.

In the stillness we will find our truth. We will find the answers. We will find direction. It may take traveling through a layer of pain and disappointment and the debris left by lost hope and shattered dreams, but, beneath them we will find ourselves, our lives and the truth that will carry us forward.

CARING FOR MOM

My mother likes to believe she's independent. Since my father died a few years ago, I have encouraged her to live with me and my family. She stubbornly refuses. She does not want to depend on, or interfere, in her children's lives. She lives instead in a retirement community, one that has taken her and my deceased father's entire life savings to afford and still requires monthly input from her five children.

Mom believes she's independent, but in reality it takes all five of us, a ton of patience and more than one glass of wine to keep this ninety eight pound woman going and she is in near perfect health. She has the ordinary annoyances of age such as poor eyesight, diminished hearing, balance issues and a less than perfect memory, but nothing major. My siblings, two brothers and two sisters, each handle the situation differently, some with more aplomb and dignity than others. There are as many ways of dealing with the care of an aging parent as there are people. My siblings and I are a microcosm that can afford a brief look at some of the ways people react.

One sister, who actively resists Mom's contrariness, restlessness and just plain stubbornness, has the misfortune (or God given challenge) of taking care of her day to day needs. Catherine lives closest to Mom and has a flexible schedule. She has taken on the task with gusto, as is her style, and has made it her full blown responsibility to do the best job possible. Mom, however, is rarely content.

"Why can't she just be happy? I do everything in my power to make her happy! I buy her plants, I take her to the doctor, and I arrange her hair appointments. The other people in her community are busy doing things and enjoying life," she continues, "Why can't she?" The anger and frustration ooze out between her words like thick molasses. Her question is a reasonable one. Mom has *always* been contrary and becomes more so with age.

Early on, I learned to give up trying to change my mother making it easier for me to accept and even come close to understanding my mother's way of handling her journey into aging. Her increasing disregard for her appearance and her disinterest in socializing make some sort of sense to me. These things are no longer priorities to her.

"Why is she wearing that ratty old thing? She has a closet full of clothes!" Catherine erupts. Most of which she bought Mom in an attempt to get her to "shape up." I understand her frustration with this issue as well.

Mom recently said, "If I had someone to wash and iron my clothes, pick them out and lay them out for me each day, I think I could live forever." I believe this reveals her growing difficulty and loss of energy to do even the smallest tasks. As each day passes even the most enjoyable activities become more difficult. It's a struggle for her to hear what's being said on TV, or to make out the words on a page. She always enjoyed reading.

A conversation with a neighbor requires her to rise above the insecurity induced by not being able to think of the words needed to express herself. "I just feel so dim-witted! These people are so smart and I can't carry on a conversation that makes any sense. Even if I have something I want to say, I can't remember the details or find the words I need." Proud of being a college graduate in a time when women didn't often go to college, it hurts her pride.

Opening a bottle of aspirin requires a pressure on the fingers that is now painful and impossible to do. She tries to bake cookies for her neighbors but can't keep track of the ingredients, often leaving one out. What she once did easily is now monumental.

My sister isn't ready, just yet, to let Mom be who she is now. It's tough to accept our mother's aging process in all its imperfection and unsightliness. Instead Catherine runs herself ragged, buying Mom clothes, cleaning and organizing her closets, all the while terrified of not making her happy. Maybe she feels she is running out of time to accomplish this feat. I try to tell her, like I repeatedly tell myself, that it is not our job to make Mom happy, a truism in all relationships. That still falls on Mom's shoulders.

Another sister, who lives in the same town with Mom, has chosen to put her own life first. "I just decided I'm not going to let her ruin my life. I'm done letting her do that," she said. She relegates Mom to a small corner of her life. She runs errands and takes her to the hairdresser, mostly to help Catherine out. She avoids as much emotional connection as possible. Sandra is not an unloving, or uncaring person. She simply has chosen to deal with Mom's aging in her own way. Maybe it's less painful for her, but I wonder if regrets will set in when Mom is gone.

My two brothers live 600 miles away away. They share responsibility for financial matters and visit or call as often as they can. They don't worry like my sisters and I do about Mom's daily happiness or psychological well-being. As long as she's relatively healthy, they keep their concerns to the practical side of matters. My brothers do all the guy things Mom dreams up for them to do when they visit and their wives send notes and pictures of great grandchildren.

My oldest brother Tom works tirelessly to gather genealogical information and old photos, documenting every item any of us possess that represents part of our heritage. Mom is the oldest living relative in either her family or my father's and she will carry a treasury of our family's history with her to the grave. Tom carries a tape recorder with him when he visits Mom, recording the anecdotes she relates about her past. The recalling and reliving of the past is something elderly people do as a means of processing their lives and letting go process.

I live three hours away and do not have to deal with Mom on a daily basis. She comes to stay with me for a week or two every few months and at Christmas. I visit her in-between. Yes, she tries my patience and I am always relieved when she goes home, but I have come to cherish our visits.

The siblings and spouses all struggle with how much responsibility they can handle, as do I, and how much time can be devoted to caring for Mom. As with all families, we carry psychological baggage and the unfinished business of all parent/child relationships. Each time she visits me though, I learn something new about her, or myself. Taking the time to sit with her and listen has helped me grow, especially in the understanding of our relationship. I know her better than I did before and it has helped me to accept her shortcomings and to see her, for who she is, not who I want her to be or think she should be. Sometimes it is difficult to just sit and chat when I have so many other things to do, especially when I hear the same story ten times, but it has made me stop and consider the aging and dying process.

It is easy to forget that our aging parents are still people, albeit difficult, cantankerous and certainly demanding people. Trite though it may sound, it is helpful to realize, and more importantly accept, that their lives are dwindling down to memories of the past as their focus on the future narrows. They are closing in to themselves, both physically and emotionally. It is time for them to look backward and evaluate. They no longer want or need to look forward and plan a future. They are not interested in replacing the twenty or forty year friendships they've lost to death.

Their story has been told and they have little need to write another chapter. They are trying to let go. We can't and shouldn't interfere with this process but rather accompany them, as we are able, on the journey.

Erik Erikson who is known as "the father of psychosocial development" believed that each of us passes through eight stages of development in our lifetime. The elderly are in the last stage that he called "Integrity vs. Despair." In this stage a person looks back over their life and evaluates whether or not it was as fulfilling as they had hoped it would be. If they affirm that it was a good life, they become ready to face death. If they cannot affirm their lives they tend to fear death.

As our parents wait for death, our gift as children and grandchildren is to accept their individual method of traveling the course and to take as much time out of our busy lives as we can to just be with them; to sit and listen to their stories, to share a meal and to give them an extra hug or two along the way. It goes without saying that their physical needs must be met, but it is their growing sense of isolation and aloneness that can be most frightening to them, especially if they are struggling to accept their lives as they've lived them. They are finding their way onto a new and unknown path that they must travel alone. We can walk with them, as far as fate allows.

If we can find our own way along this often difficult passageway, we will be better for it. We do need to weigh our own emotional and physical strength and our ability to cope with the demands and find a way to make it as comfortable for ourselves as possible. I try not to judge my siblings for their way of caring for Mom. I can't say I don't wish sometimes they'd see things more my way, as no doubt they do about me as well. I understand that we are all at different places in our emotional development and have different life pressures. We do the best we can.

The most important part of this process for me isn't the care-taking, the errands and chores that won't change the outcome. I want to accompany her along her journey and do what I can to help her face and accept the process. The chores still need to be done, but they are just added to my to-do-list and no longer carry the emotional weight they once did. When viewed this way "taking care of Mom" allows time to sit down with her and have a cup of tea without any expectations.

PUPPY LOVE

There is something in the DNA of college age offspring that prompts them to bring a pet home. Just as they're wrapping up final exams at the end of the last semester, of their last year of college, it happens. Right smack at the exact moment they realize they haven't the first clue what they are doing with the rest of their lives, they take a detour.

They *say* they are anxious to be on their own and even use this conviction as bait to get our approval of the forty pound adoptee. I believe they are hanging on to dependent status as long as they can. They can't, however, seem to fight their natural instinct to multiply, even as they are clearly ill equipped to care for themselves.

They can't cope with a pet. You knew this when you said no the first time they asked and they shouted at you indignantly that they weren't a child anymore! Invariably, we silly parents acquiesce and the stray moves in. The trouble begins, just as you knew it would.

For some reason the offspring feel justified in thrusting the critter on the entire family as they continue to go about their lives as if absolutely nothing has changed. They don't hesitate to turn to Mom and Dad to bail them out when the pet sitter they swear they contacted falls through for the week they plan to be at the beach with their friends.

We are in dangerous waters as well. Sitting on the precipice of a major change in our lives, we swear we are as eager and ready to let go of our kids as they are of us, while we silently cling to their need of us. It is a dangerous situation.

Out of misguided compassion for our kid...or more likely for the crazed pet, we lend a hand...and then two...and then it happens.

The eager lad who brought the adorable critter home has suddenly become *too* busy...and, Mom and Dad...half heartedly at first...kicking and screaming...relent. Then, to make matters worse, they are afflicted. They fall in love with the puppy like it were their first grandchild.

It is programmed into our DNA as well. I've seen it happen too often for it to be merely chance. Just as Mom is beginning to feel the angst of her empty nest, the original object of her affection gives her a replacement. Perhaps it makes it easier for both of them to walk away from the bond they have come to depend so much on.

The adult-child subconsciously knows that Mom needs a substitute and provides one, albeit quite without asking. He needs to feel Mom is happy so he can let go. Too much psychology? Perhaps.

The up side of all of this is that Mom gets to hold the wiggling bundle of fluff in her arms, so preoccupied with his cuteness, that she barely notices her son walk out of the door, this time for good.

THE SWITFNESS OF TIME

I don't suppose it's possible to walk through life totally conscious of what we're doing...but if we could, I think we would choose not do three quarters of what we do. I think, instead, we'd work harder to do the few things that are really important to us, not those mindless, soul numbing activities we so often opt to do instead.

Every now and then I feel such swift movement of time. Like, wow, where did those ten years go? With my nose so close to the grindstone, acting and mostly reacting to all of life's events, big chunks of time seem to slip by almost imperceptibly.

I feel a sense of loss when I came up for air, at the opportunities missed, the choices I maybe should have made and didn't because of fear or lack of foresight...or lack of time to think. I am grateful for so much and have experienced so much...but, ah, there was *so* much more in each of those moments and hours now gone!

If there is just one thing I could impart to my children and the young people of the world, it would be to pay attention. Pay *close* attention to each moment and get the most from life. It goes by so fast. Sometimes it hits me like a ton of bricks.

CARETAKING DECISIONS

My siblings and I continue to care for my mother and we struggle with an increasing number of decisions regarding her care. The five of us, with five opinions and five different ways of seeing things, struggle to reach a consensus. We've managed to be amicable so far, but the stress and uncertainty is beginning to stretch the ties that bind!

As I've mentioned, I wanted to bring my mother home to live with my husband and me shortly. She wanted that too, but my siblings disagreed and encouraged her to stay in the retirement home. They wanted her to stay in town near my sisters lived rather than be moved a state away.

Now, as her capabilities diminish, we are taking turns caring for her. I travel three plus hours and take my turn three or four days a week. My brothers still only come every few months, mostly on an as needed basis. It has become costly for them to make repeated trips.

Though my sisters live in town, they did not want to be responsible for her full time care. It was decided that she should be moved from her apartment to Assisted Living where she would receive more help and supervision. The decision sounded reasonable at the time and under normal circumstances it might have been an easy thing to do. But, nothing is simple when you are dealing with the elderly.

I was fearful that all the upheaval and change would only make matters worse and so it did. Her confusion has increased and she doesn't seem to know what has happened. There is no joy in being right in such a situation.

Retirement communities claim to provide more than adequate supervision and care and tout "Assisted Living" as an ideal solution for those who need extra care. Even the nicest facilities such as the one my mother is in, provide less care than most of us want for our loved ones. They always seem to be short handed and many of the caregivers leave something to be desired.

We hired a full time aide to fill in when one of us could not be with Mom. I can't help but wonder why we are paying for extra care at the facility, for additional private care, and making sure that one of us is with her for a good portion of each day, when the same amount of effort and money, or less, would pay for around the clock nursing care in one of our homes. It's a myth to think you forget about a loved one when you go home at night and leave them behind. You worry just the same.

The wheels of change keep turning and we keep trying to do the best we can for her. It's only been a few days since the move. I'm hoping she'll adjust. When I spoke to her yesterday, she was barely coherent and scarcely uttered a word. Last week she was lucid and conversant.

STRESSED OUT – YOU CAN SURVIVE!

"How are you coping with your mother's failing health?" a friend recently asked.

My initial instinct was to reply "I'm not!" Most of the time, I feel exhausted, sleepless and drained. Of course I actually said something like, "I'm surviving".

Later as I thought about her question, and my answer, I came to the realization that in dire circumstances, when life's stresses are mounting beyond what we can comfortably handle, surviving *is* coping and sometimes coping better than we give ourselves credit for.

We have all read a million articles on how to deal with stress. We are regularly advised to: eat right, exercise and take time for ourselves. However, we are *not* usually reading these articles while we are in the middle of the crisis, then we don't have time to read! In more relaxed times we may ponder the advice and perhaps even dabble in a few healthy behaviors, telling ourselves we will definitely take the advice to heart when we need it.

One morning we wake up and the time has come. We are caring for an elderly parent as our siblings tug and pull at one another; our college aged children are dabbling in drugs or alcohol while draining our bank accounts; our spouse has developed a heart condition or other physical ailment or is in the middle of a career crisis; middle aged weight gain and unruly hormones wreak havoc with our self image and render us sluggish, sleepless and dimwitted; we're in a career we no longer find fulfilling or the fast pace of technology has left us feeling inadequate; our best friend is struggling with an abusive husband and a messy divorce and calls us daily for moral support. Before we know it a level of stress is upon us that we didn't even know was possible. It's too late to put coping techniques into place. We needed them *yesterday!*

If you are one of the lucky people who have developed self-discipline, you heed good advice when you read it and have the coping strategies in place when a crisis arrives. You deserve kudos. You will fare better because of it. The only thing left for you to do is to hang on to those habits with a death grip as you ride out the chaos life has handed you. Pat yourself on the back as well because these habits carry their positive affects forward and have done their job already by making your body, mind and soul stronger. You will come through your crisis less ravaged and far less depleted than most.

If, however, you're like me and few things ever become real habits, coping and dealing means something quite different. We have to figure out how to survive while in the middle of drowning and there is little access to air. But I'm here to tell you, it is possible and it will be okay.

Often it is the little things we do that add up to survival. Tiny steps and small changes can keep us afloat. We do not need to berate ourselves for struggling and feeling the pain of life. We do need to grab hold of a life raft and get through it the best we can. And that's okay. In fact, it's often more than okay. It's heroic.

I found such a life raft this past year when I picked up and began reading my copy of Sarah Ban Breathnach's, Simple Abundance, Daybook of Comfort and Joy. It had been sitting in my nightstand for almost eight years untouched. Ironically, it was a gift from a friend who is going through a difficult divorce. Little did she know then that she was giving me a tool to help me help her cope now!

I dusted off the cover and began to read. For those who are unfamiliar with this gem, it is a book of daily readings to inspire us to a life of what the author calls "simple abundance". When I picked it up it was June and not January where the book begins, but after confronting my psychological feng shui, I dove straight into the middle of the book. I have been reading it, *almost* every day, since. January did finally arrive and I was able to finally begin at the beginning! I have since come to realize that reading this book was one of the many small steps I barely noticed I was taking that helped me cope and survive the unremitting assault on my sanity and well being.

Each daily reading in Simple Abundance can be read in less than five minutes. They are my daily touchstone of sanity and help keep me grounded and in touch with what is truly important in life. (I suggest leaving your copy in the bathroom – we all spend at least a few minutes there each day!) In addition to the daily words of wisdom, the author suggests small things you can do each day to bring your life into focus. Five minutes with <u>Simple Abundance</u> provides manageable bites of coping strategies that can be swallowed even in the midst of a crisis.

Ban Breathnach suggests starting a "blessings journal". Every day, write five things in the journal for which you are grateful. You are swallowing a survival vitamin with each entry, even if you can only manage once or twice a week rather than every day. I personally have a hit or miss relationship with my "blessings journal" but my hit or miss has added up over the months. I recently sat down and read over my entries. Beyond the daily exercise of making the entries, reading them again gave me perspective as well. I was lifted up by the thread of gratitude I had expressed. It was personal and real. This small exercise strengthens and informs our lives. Try it!

While I have not had the time, money and self-discipline to join a gym, I have learned and know with unfailing certainty that exercise makes me feel better. Whenever I have the opportunity I go for a walk. The fresh air clears my mind, the aerobic exercise pumps up my endorphins and I survive another day. If I don't feel I can afford the time for a walk I acknowledge this and work to enhance the aerobic intensity of chores, e.g. cleaning house, yard work, etc.

In addition, I have allowed myself the time and luxury of friendship. It doesn't seem as if it should be a luxury and yet in this fast paced world of duty and obligation, when we tend to put our extra energy into family and career, it is easy to let friendship fall to the bottom of our list of priorities. I'm not suggesting a full social calendar. Just one friend, with whom you can share your joys and sorrows on a very regular basis, other than your spouse, can make a difference.

This was a hard lesson for me to learn and it may not have happened if my crazy friend going through her divorce hadn't started calling me every day. I am one of those self-sacrificing women who find it much easier to give than to receive but in doing so I developed one heck of a friendship with a wonderful woman who gives me as much as I need in understanding and support. I got through a few life crises without her but I am faring much better this time around with her in my life.

I learned one other little gem on this journey and that is to allow time for laughter and time for tears. One of the items I added to my "blessings journal" is the four hour drive to and from my mother's place. It is no longer the arduous routine it once was as I have come to look forward to the time alone. It is a time when I can let all the feelings I hold at bay to come crashing in. Invariably I spend a major portion of every trip crying. I listen to music that I love, I relax, and my feelings surface. My psyche has the space it needs to experience the pain I have kept unconsciously at bay.

I've have learned to dispense with makeup while I'm traveling and to take plenty of tissues and a bottle of water. Crying makes me thirsty! I have come to see this process as very therapeutic and healing. There are so many things in life we cannot control, but we can survive and letting ourselves feel our pain and sorrow helps us to survive.

Laughter is a little harder to come by, but when I have time I watch inane sitcoms or Comedy Central rather than crime dramas or the news. I also rent DVD's and CD's of my favorite comedians. An hour of laughter is at least as good for us if not better than an hour of tears.

We must accept our humanity and our tendency to be unprepared. It is largely a myth that we can be prepared for life's difficulties, but doing the little things that give us strength to go on is what coping is all about. Sometimes coping is just making it through the day.

EXPECTATIONS

I am dreading the upcoming visit to my mother's, my first since her move to assisted living. The decision to keep her in an institution, albeit a nice one, seemed to make some sort of practical sense to everyone but me. From an emotional standpoint I find it devastating. I feel down to my toes that Mom should be at home with family.

She fell right after Thanksgiving, and although uninjured, except for bruises, her general health seems to suddenly be declining. My sisters and I cared for her 24/7 through the holiday season. We hoped that she would recover enough to be left alone again, but there has been little real progress in that respect.

Worn thin by the demands of the situation, it seemed time to accept the room that opened up where, theoretically, she would receive regular help. There was no way of knowing when another room would become available.

Now, instead of a two bedroom, two bath apartment she has a large single room with space for a sitting area and a bathroom. I will not be able to stay with her as I always have and will stay across town with my sister instead. I feel more like a visitor and less like a daughter.

In her new living quarters she is supposed to have help whenever she needs it. It seems, however, that the assistance only comes if Mom asks for it and she can't or won't ask for it! As a result, my sisters feel someone needs to be with her much of the time, defeating the purpose of move itself. They have set up a schedule so that either the aide or one of my sisters is with her until she is asleep at night.

The people who live in Assisted Living are not people needing a little help getting in bed at night. They are, in reality, in pretty bad shape. Most barely speak, many can't walk, or hear, or see. Despite the hype, there is little potential for Mom to make a connection that might help her feel comfortable. She had many friends who lived near her apartment that checked in on her every day when she was there. Now it is harder for them to visit.

I have just recovered from the flu myself, but I'm back on my feet and ready to see firsthand what is going on. I have to admit, I am still angry about how things have turned out, but I will do my best not to show it. At this point it would serve no purpose.

My mother's belongings, those things that could not be used in her new room, have been moved to my sister's garage. They await my arrival to help with the sorting and distributing...another downsizing event. There have been several.

THE NEW DIGS

When I arrived at my mother's new living quarters, I found she was doing about the same as when I saw her last. Apart from the fact that she speaks less and less she is mobile and healthy. It is obvious that my brother and sister put a lot of effort into making her room look and feel homey. She is well cared for by my sisters and the aide.

Mom is still confused about the move and tells me over and over, "someone has cut my room in half and I don't know what they've done with the other half!" She complains to me that "no one asked *me* if I liked this room".

She is worried about many little things, like not having money to tip the hairdresser, and big, such as what happened to all her things. She has always felt comfortable complaining to me about such things while preferring to keep my sisters in the dark about her dissatisfaction. I try to answer her questions without upsetting her more. It's not an easy task because the truth of the matter is she was moved without her consent and had absolutely no say in what she brought with her or what was sent to storage.

Most of the time she just goes along with what everyone tells her to do. She struggles to make even the simplest of decisions so it is easier. On a good day, she recognizes that she has relinquished control of her life and she is angry and belligerent. She doesn't like feeling helpless and out of control. On good days she wants back what she lost and to make her own decisions. I don't blame her.

Her monthly living expenses have gone up dramatically and we all wonder how long we can afford to keep her where she is, though moving her again hardly seems an option.

My sisters and I spent the better part of two days going through my mother's belongings that had been carted to my sister's garage. In spite of the conflict and stress we all were feeling, we laughed until we cried, as we reminisced about our childhood.

My sister dangled one of my mother's little nature treasures from her finger, "What on God's green earth is this?" It looked a bit like some sort of wood nymph, not even close to something either sister would have in their homes! We laughed until tears came to our eyes, not because it was all that funny, but because we all needed an emotional release.

Mom had hung on to some of the craziest things. We pulled out item after item, many of which were over a half century old and of no particular value to anyone but Mom ...and in some odd way to us. So many memories. What do you do with things that have sentimental value but are neither something you would display or use?

We each are grieving in our own way We are trying to let go as we know it is inevitable and struggling to make peace with the both the past and the present. We are ages fifty-five, fifty-nine and sixty two and we are all facing the challenges of aging, both physical and emotional. In the midst of our sorrow it is good to find common ground and connection to two people who had lived childhoods as similar to mine as any other.

I had been nervous about the visit. The reality was different than what I had anticipated. It was not so bad and my anger over decisions made slipped away. The next visit will be a little bit easier I think.

MOTHER'S DAY

I'm spending Mother's Day with Mom, sitting beside her hospital bed. Three days ago she fell and broke her upper thigh bone; only a few short weeks after her move to her new quarters in assisted living. She is frail and the dementia has taken a deeper bite out of her awareness. Miraculously she has survived surgery, unlike my father who coincidently broke the exact same bone seven years ago only to die two hours after surgery.

For four days now I have been here, by her side, as she clings to life. I drip water into her mouth, moisturize her lips, and keep her oxygen tube in place which she tries to pull off every five minutes when she is awake. When she is alert enough to talk I laugh at the nonsensical things she says because she smiles when she says them. When she cries out in pain, I cry with her.

I am so grateful for my mother. As much as her contrary, mysterious ways have agitated and annoyed me over the years, I am a better person because she loved me...and loved life. As I gaze upon her ninety pound, five foot frame, I wonder how such a little woman could have had such a huge influence on me all these years.

Each day, she takes one step forward and one step back in her recovery, the emotional roller coaster taking its toll on all of us.

Tomorrow I leave her side and ready myself for my return trip home to North Carolina for a few days. I don't want to leave, but I desperately need the break. I will pass the torch to my sister. We will hug goodbye, each silently struggling with "what's next?"

It's hard not to wonder why Mom has to suffer so much at this point in her life. There is no happy outcome, no reward for the suffering from an earthly perspective. Still, we have to move forward and make each decision as if she will recover and live forever.

What does recovery look like for a woman of ninety seven? She could barely walk before she fell. Now her bones are soft and the pins holding them together uncertain – there cannot possibly be enough of a recovery for her to walk again. Or can there? We want to make the right decisions as plan her future care. But what is the right choice? Should we minimize her suffering and not worry about rehabilitation? Or is that giving up? If we persist and act proactively could she have several years ahead of her? Or is it time?

In reality, it's not our decision. It's hers and it's God's – we can only walk beside her and hold her hand. She will do what she will do and we will love her to the end. We will take each step as if she will live forever, providing all the medical benefits available. She has not yet given up and neither will we.

UNEASY CHOICES

Caring for Mom has taken so many twists and turns over the last five years. As her ability to function decreases, our involvement increases. It is a difficult process, but most of us go through it at one time or another in our lives.

I've come to believe that the most important thing a caregiver can do is learn to give up control over things that cannot be controlled. I have been able to watch my sisters from the vantage point of a slight geographical distance as they run in circles trying to do "the right thing" for Mom. No sooner do they get everything "under control" than something changes, but isn't that just life? There is only so much we can control and death is not one of them.

After just moving Mom from her apartment to assisted living we are now considering moving her to Healthcare where she will receive medical supervision as she recovers from her broken leg. Each time we face a decision we ask the same questions.

Should we move her? What should we do with her stuff? Should we keep it or get rid of it? Should we give up her room or apartment, or will she recover enough to go back? We want to be certain that the decision we make is the right one because there is no going back. There is also no way of knowing what the right decision is. We do not have a clue what tomorrow will bring. The only option is to jump in and live with the consequences.

The decisions are not easier for me, but distance has given me more of an opportunity to reflect and regroup between visits. I try to use this vantage point to provide support, encouragement and perspective to my sisters. They are carrying the greater day to day burden and perspective is harder for them to come by.

We each have a unique purpose in our families. If we can claim our gifts and accept them with grace and compassion, we can then give to the rest of the family members something they may need. I may be able to offer perspective, but my next oldest sister is an organizer and she has been a God send to the rest of us. It all works out in the end if we let it and resist the urge to fight it.

INDEPENDENCE VS. DEPENDENCE

I've been thinking a lot about independence and dependence since my last visit with my mother. How do we learn to respect the need for both in ourselves and in others? We come into this world totally dependent on others and often leave the same way. In the middle years between birth and death we live with the illusion that we are independent. And yet, are we really? At the very least, we are dependent on others for love and support, and usually a whole lot more.

In recent decades, we have come to overvalue independence in this country. We think we should and must be able to deal with life comfortably and effectively without asking for support. In fact, we think that there is something wrong with us if we do have needs. This kind of thinking works against love and community and ultimately leaves us feeling isolated and alone.

Historically, women have been viewed as dependent people. Our generation has worked very hard to prove to the world and ourselves that we can stand on our own two feet and not only survive, but thrive. In truth, the women of yesteryear were quite independent, just in a different way.

There is a certain strength and comfort in allowing ourselves to rely on another person, while knowing we can take care of ourselves if needed. What would life be like if we could not give to others? If we insist on being totally independent we do not give our loved ones the opportunity to give to us. We deprive ourselves of something we need and them as well.

Mom has become dependent on her children. She took care of us until we were able to stand on our own and then she took care of my father for twenty some years after he had a stroke. After his death, she had only herself to look after, an uncomfortable departure from a lifetime of giving. During much of that time she relied on us for nothing more than the love we chose to give her.

Now, she has lost the ability to care for herself. Fortunately, she is not cognizant enough to understand how dependent she has become. She would not like it. Every now and then, she seems to realize what is happening and her frustration is evident. She still wants her independence even as she knows she is not capable of having it. Age puts us in some terrible binds.

I try to give her the freedom to make at least small decisions. I encourage her to decide whether she wants oatmeal for breakfast or an egg or whether to sit on the deck or in the living room for her afternoon tea. When I help her get dressed I ask her if she would like to wear a sweater. Sometimes it's the small things that make a difference.

Caring for her has been a blessing to me. I don't mind giving back something of what she has given to me. Too often it does not seem like near enough.

When I reach her age or condition, I know I am going to hate being dependent on my children, or anyone else. I hope I can remember how I am feeling now and allow others to give to me. I would like to be able to remember, that in giving, we receive, and let people give to me. I'm not very good at it now so I think I'd better start practicing!

When we start to resent our dependency it may help to remember that it is just part of the way this crazy life works. Rather than fighting it, we can just lean into it and try a little harder to be grateful for the gift that is being given to us.

SAYING GOODBYE TO MOM

My brother-in-law called yesterday. He asked me how my mother was doing. I thought a minute, searching for the right words to describe her current state.

"She's dying." They were the only words that seemed to fit. Silence stood between us for a moment. "I'm sorry," I continued, suddenly realizing my words were probably less comfortable for him than they had become for me.

My mother is five days away from her ninety- seventh birthday. A picture of health throughout most of her life she has been on a steady decline over the last six weeks. She still has no nameable ailments, apart from her slowly healing leg, but the number of hours she sleeps has increased steadily and her heart rate has decreased. She is quiet and withdrawn. She knows us but no longer connects emotionally but on rare occasions. She is increasingly confused and needs around the clock care. Yes, she is dying.

As my two sisters and I walk this path with her, we do our best to provide for her daily care. We made the decision to move her to Healthcare. It was the only real option when she was released from the hospital. She cannot walk and must be lifted in and out of bed.

In Healthcare she receives medical supervision and aides make sure she is cared for around the clock. We have asked our aide to stay on and we continue to take turns visiting with Mom.

The caretakers and staff barely know she's there. They have so many others to attend to and quickly fall out of sight when we are there, which is a majority of the time. The staff seems shorthanded and their expertise minimal.

We are afraid to leave her in their care and continue to do much of it ourselves, asking for help only when it is necessary. We want her to have the best and don't like it when she is neglected. It is difficult, tiring, stressful and emotionally draining but it is our gift to Mom, to each other and to us. The process is helping us grieve and let go, each in our own way, little by little as she continues to let go of us.

The first weeks in Healthcare, I kept thinking, "wait, I'm not ready". My sister went into overdrive making sure Mom got out of bed and dressed each day, whether she wanted to or not. She scheduled doctor's appointments, hair dresser's appointments and activities, anything to keep her going. My sister was not ready either.

As each day passes we are realizing and beginning to accept that we are not in control. This is my mother's journey. It is her choice to stay or go. We can walk beside her, but we cannot control the outcome.

It is hard for us to give up control, particularly when death is the certain end, but it is us with an important life lesson. We do not have the control in life we like to think we have. Quite often we can only go along with what life brings our way and choose instead to let it mold and shape us and provide depth and meaning to our days, past, present and future.

I will be leaving shortly to return to my Mom's side; to hold her hand one more time as we take another step in our journey together.

DIGNITY
A SHORT STORY

"Mom! What are you doing?" I called from her bedroom doorway. I had just arrived to take her out for the morning. She stood facing her old mahogany dresser, her back to me; studying a framed photo she held in her hand, one she had taken from the massive collection that littered the top of dresser.

A turtleneck top hung loosely over her slight frame, unwilling to shield the soft, sagging mounds of her buttocks or spindly legs covered only in loose flesh worn thin by time. One foot was quite properly attired in a knee sock and stood haughtily beside the other unsheathed and forlorn.

She turned slightly and looked at me blankly.

"I don't know," she said, as if wondering herself. Her gaze drifted back to the photo she was now surprised to find in her hand.

"Do you need help getting dressed?" I asked.

An image of her petite figure, dressed perfectly in a hand-tailored suit, rousted itself from my memory; her hat in place, a small, neat, purse slipped carefully over one arm, her gloves in the same hand, thrust forth purposefully; she was ready for church.

Her ever so slightly shrill voice echoed from the past, "Dorothy! Your father's in the car!" A lifelong Episcopalian and a woman proud of her English heritage, she carried herself with dignity. She attended all church functions remotely academic, as if to remind herself, and perhaps others, of the college degree she had earned though never used. She was the mother of five. That had been her full time job. Yet, a college degree was an exceptional accomplishment for a woman in the 1920's and she was deeply proud of it, though she never said as much.

The church, a big enough world for her, was her life outside of the family.

Waving the picture she still held, she took a wobbly step. I reached for her just as she found her balance. I dropped my hand. Still clinging ferociously to her bits of independence, she jabbed a finger at the photo. It was a well worn photo of my brother's son at two, some twenty years ago shortly before his death -- "You know this guy?" she asked, "quite certain that I did not. "*Dead*...just a *baby*...tsk", she clucked, a long forgotten tear resting in the corner of her eye.

"Yes, Mom, I remember," I said quietly. "I've laid clothes out for you." I dug through the pile on her bed and pulled out her panties. I held them out to her. She liked to dress herself as much as possible.

Struck suddenly by a memory whisper, her eyes widened, "Oh, those!" She sucked in air, as her mouth few open. Her free hand rose to cover it, the other tugged on the hem of her shirt to cover her nakedness. The mortifying awareness of her current state washed over her.

She scowled and shook her head, a familiar gesture that meant disappointment or anger. We never knew which. "Oh" she groaned, her voice fading as vacant confusion replaced the shock. I exchanged the pants for the picture, pretending not to notice her predicament.

I sat beside her on the bed as she worked them up over her cold skin. I did not move to help her even as every fiber of my being resisted the bondage. I continued to wait as she pulled her slacks on next.

At last properly dressed, a process started over an hour ago, she seemed my mother again.

"Would you like to go for a walk?" I asked, hopefully.

"I'm tired," she said eyeing her pillow, her head tilting and her eyes closing. "Maybe later...bed looks *so* good." She leaned slowly toward the spread covered pillow. Finding its support at last, she sighed, her eyes closing tightly. I lifted her shoed feet up onto the bed. Unable to take her shoes off so soon after putting them on, I left them in place. I covered her with a light blanket and tucked her in like I had my children. I leaned in and kissed her cheek.

"I love you, Mom." I stood a moment, awash with emotion. "We'll walk later."

"SUNDOWNING"

Sundowning is a pattern of behavior in elderly people who have dementia or Alzheimer's where they become agitated and confused after the sun goes down at night.

My mother has exhibiting this behavior in varying degrees for about six months. It can be perplexing and unnerving at first but is easier to deal with when you know what is happening. There are ways to minimize it.

The first time I experienced sundowning was one evening while I was visiting Mom before she moved from her apartment. We sat together, side by side, eating dinner and watching TV. She turned to me and asked, "Where is your Dad?"

My father has been dead for eight years. She was quite herself and lucid during the day at that point and I was caught completely off guard. I didn't know how to respond. Should I tell her the truth or go along with her delusion? I stumbled my way through it that night reminding her that he had died. She looked surprised and upset that no one had told her. The question resurfaced again and again in addition to others.

Sometimes I merely said, "He's out" and she would go back to what she was doing. Other times she would push and insist until I told her the truth and then she would cry, each time experiencing his death like it was the first time.

Dementia is usually caused by illness or mini strokes that have damaged a person's brain cells. *Sundowning* is thought to occur due to the correspondent damage of a person's circadian rhythms, the internal clock that regulates the body's physiological activities over a twenty four hour period.

There are several things you can do to try and minimize the effects of *sundowning*.

- Keep the person active and awake during the day as much as possible. It makes it easier for them to fall asleep in the evening.
- Plan activities during morning hours and keep the afternoon activities calm and simple.
- When possible make sure the person receives morning sunlight and increase interior light before dusk.
- Keep your loved ones life and surroundings simple and uncluttered. A sudden change can make it worse.
- Sometimes confusion can be caused or aggravated by dehydration or hunger. Often the elderly turn away from food and drink, increasing the likelihood of deficiencies.

I WISH

I wish I could walk with Mom in her garden...just one more time, arm in arm, absorbing her love for nature. She loved anything that lives and breathes...loves still. I don't want to have to talk about her in the past tense just yet. Though she is almost gone, she is still present.

I want to hug her tight...just one more time...and feel her hug me back...her love infusing my heart with reassurance. I miss that already. It seems an eternity since she had the strength to hug me back...even though it's only been a few months.

I wish I could tell her the stories of my life...those things that have been sitting inside me in the place reserved for sharing with her. She didn't always understand, but she always listened. She always cared. I miss that so much and will miss it even more when she's gone.

It is so hard sometimes to walk this life day after day, letting go one by one of the people we love...the people that provided the foundation for our being...the people that loved us unconditionally.

I want to say to her, "Go, it is okay"... but a big part of me says, "No, please don't go". I wonder if that is why she clings to life, she feels me here holding on. I want to be ready to let her go, even as I know I never will.

Dad is waiting for you Mom. I just know he is. You will be safe. I promise. Just reach out from heaven and touch me when you get there, so I know you have arrived safe and sound. Tell me that God does exist and that He will be waiting for me when my time comes.

I'll miss you Mom. I love you.

LETTING GO

Letting go is never easy. It's hard to say goodbye to someone you've loved your whole life. Most of us know what that's like by this point in our lives. It never gets any easier no matter how many times we practice the skill. We may learn to bear the sadness and sorrow a little bit better each time. But letting go? That never gets any easier.

We search for ways to keep the memories of our loved ones alive after they're gone. That is the beauty of memories. They are a gift that buoys us up and opens the floodgates of grief. Every time we have a lovely memory of someone we've lost we should thank God for the blessing of memory, even if it brings tears to our eyes and a pain in our hearts.

I sat beside my mother today, outside by a small man-made pond with fountain and flowers. It is a beautiful little spot crafted in the corner of a courtyard right outside the suffocating walls of the health care facility where she is now staying.

She did not acknowledge me when I arrived an hour earlier. I found her sleeping in her chair in the dining hall and promptly wheeled her out to sit by the pond. If she was going to sleep through her last moments on earth she was not going to be forced to do it over a bowl of cold oatmeal. How she would hate to die that way!

We sat together by the pond not speaking or communicating in any obvious way, but I remembered the many conversations we shared before she drifted away.

It was a glorious hour of contemplation and sadness as I watched, as if through her eyes, as the birds played in the fountain and the roses bloomed nearby. Even though she is not yet gone, she is in so many ways already gone. She sits on the precipice of death as I sit beside her still trying to enjoy those things she once enjoyed, a vicarious presence. How I wished she could let go, in that spot, side by side with nature where she belonged. It is not perfect, but as close as she'll get now. I'd rather she not die in a strange hospital bed in a dark room, alone.

I don't have any control over her dying and so I sit beside her and wait with her for the moment when it's time...when the almost memories will become real memories. I hope they lift me up to touch her face again, at least in my heart.

ONE MORE MOMENT

I am struck by our need as women -- mothers, daughters, and friends -- to nurture -- to feed and comfort. One of the hardest things about watching my mother die is not being able to give her a sip of water or a bite of Jell-O. She does not want to eat and forcing her to do so is prolonging the inevitable, or so we have been told.

She is sleeping now and not interested in waking. It's hard to sit beside her, knowing our hours together are numbered. I want to hear her talk to me again, to laugh or cry or hold one another. In reality, that time has passed and there is nothing left for me to do but wait with her.

She no longer responds when I touch her face or hold her hand. I can't stop wanting to give her a drink or a taste of pudding and yet I know it is my need not hers. I need to feed her, to care for her, to bring her back to life. She no longer cares about earthly sustenance. She is letting go and it's so hard to comprehend when you're among the living.

I understood the dying process when I read the popular book by Elizabeth Kubler-Ross, <u>On Death and Dying</u>. It made perfect sense to me. It was a process, like any other in life. I was not yet thirty at the time. What did I *really* know of death? Now, sitting beside a woman I've loved so long, it's quite a different matter.

I allow my intellect to take control of my emotions and I don't try to feed her anymore. I play soft music and listen to Lawrence Welk as I needlepoint in the chair at the foot of her bed, trying to believe it makes a difference to her that I am there. It makes a difference to me.

My sister commented to me earlier in the day, "I have such a hard time separating how I know Mom used to feel about things from how she might be feeling now. She would have hated the indignity of sleeping at the dining table."

I don't believe her dignity matters to her any longer. It only matters to us. We are doing all we can to keep her dignity intact as she passes from this world to the next...to hold her hand and walk with her as far as we are allowed to go.

THE DIFFICULTY OF NOT KNOWING

Today my mother opened her eyes a bit and tried to speak. She only connected with me for a brief second and then turned away. The Physical Therapist said that before I arrived she answered several questions and took a sip or two of juice. It's so confusing. When she shows any sign of life I want to jump to action. It's so hard not knowing. You begin to question if comfort care is the right thing to do. Are we simply starving her to death? Would a trip to the hospital with IVs, etc. bring her out of this? It was just a virus...on top of a broken leg...on top of being ninety-seven. Of course, she's dehydrated now and a lack of fluids can cause fever. All preludes to death if she does not decide to live. She has always had such a hard time making decisions. How will she makes this one? But this last decision has to be hers.

When she's quiet and sleeping I'm resolved to let her be. When she suffers or opens her eyes I oscillate between morphine and food. I also struggle with decisions that face me now, each one seems harder than the last knowing her life is at stake.

The care givers are good and supportive but each has his or her own angle -- and in the end no one knows for sure. It's up to me. Or is it? My sisters are not around; my brothers are out of state. I don't know why they don't want to be with her now. I am glued to her side. I don't want to leave her alone, though I find the uncertainty almost unbearable. If I only knew the right choice was to do nothing, I would gladly sit and hold her hand for as long as it took without hesitation or complaint. It's the uncertainty that makes it so difficult. The pain of losing her is enough. Why must I question if what I'm doing or not doing has the power to make a difference?

EXHAUSTION

I am overwhelmed with exhaustion. I put one foot in front of the other each day and seem to move forward. I do and say all the things I'm supposed to do and say, but deep inside I want to lie down and sleep for a month. I want to empty my mind and my heart and find a quiet place to rest.

Falling asleep is difficult as images of my mother's frail frame and sunken eyes remain burned in my memory. I sleep soundly once I've managed to nod off but awaken with the heaviness of the day ahead.

I am fortunate that I do freelance work and can take as much time as I need to be with Mom. I sit with her each morning but I take refuge for a few hours each afternoon in an Internet café where I lose myself in work. I return to her side at dinner time and stay with her until she's settled in for the night. It has become a routine. The respite in the afternoon keeps me going, but I miss my home, my bed and the comfort of my husband's arms.

When I arrived this morning, Mom was sleeping heavily. They had given her pain medicine but I was assured they had not yet started the morphine that will surely usher in the end. Though she cannot tell us, I think she aches from being in bed so long and she has a low grade fever.

The aide helped me get her changed into fresh clothes and clean sheets. I cradle Mom's lifeless body in my arms as she does not wake up even as the woman works her clothes onto her limp limbs.

Mom's arms are like twigs, her flesh thin and loose. Her lips are dry her leg swollen from the surgery. I am grateful she sleeps through the indignities to which she is being subjected. The aid is gentle and kind and speaks to her even though Mom no longer seems to hear. I am startled by the realization of how much like an infant Mom has become.

She is settled and comfortable when it's time for me to leave. The sitter arrives to take my place. She has been with my mother over a year now. She too seems anxious "to do" something. I try to tell her not to worry.

"Just sit with her," I say. "You can leave her now and then if you need a break. She doesn't need much from us now."

I wonder how people can bear the dying process when the one who is dying is a child, or a spouse or a young person, someone who has not had the full life that Mom has had. I don't think I could, at least not today.

I don't always feel pain and sadness. Sometimes I'm surprised when I'm not with her to feel it is just an ordinary day, that is until the exhaustion and loneliness creep in and remind me that Mom will be leaving soon.

*Stain glass window donated to
Christ Chruch, Suffern, New York by
Edward & Frances Hoffman*

July 5, 2008

My mother passed away on July 3rd, just in time to join my father for his birthday on the 4th. She went at three a.m. when we had all gone home to sleep. I am so grateful that I was able to spend her last days with her. I hope that I was of some comfort to her in her last difficult moments. I told her many times during the week how much I loved her and assured her that her way was clear.

It was a relief to head back home for a few days, to get some sleep and regroup before going back for the memorial service. I miss her and my heart aches for what I have lost, but I know she is in a better place.

Frances Anne Wickersham Hoffman

Born: 1-13-1911

Died: 7-3-2008

RESPONDING TO GRIEF

I mentioned to a friend the other day that I was surprised that I had barely cried at my mother's funeral. I had sobbed at my father's funeral and I was much closer to my mother. I had always been certain that I would know the minute she died...like I always knew when she was about to call me or was trying to reach me. I did not feel her go...she chose to stay out of reach. My friend responded to my comment by saying, "grief often comes upon us when we least expect it".

As a young adult I felt connected to my emotions. I cried when I felt hurt and I slammed doors when I was angry, but the older I get the less my emotions seem to coincide with my behavior. It's a good thing, I suppose. A fifty something woman really shouldn't be slamming doors. I guess I've learned to cope and that is convenient, but sometimes, like now, it is disconcerting.

I returned to my sister's home last week, where I had stayed the last weeks of my mother's life. She was out of town and I was house sitting and taking care of loose ends.

I love my sister's home. It's comfortable and homey. Unlike our childhood home, she has everything, including a pantry to die for, filled with cookies, M&M's and chips. She had *five* gallons of Bryer's ice cream in her freezer! Best of all is her dog Maggie, a beautiful, sweet, loving golden retriever and a wonderful companion.

I sorted through my mother's clothes and the last of her household items. I washed and packaged them up for distribution to family members and donation. I did not cry as I sniffed her favorite sweater and smelled the last scent of her. I wondered if I should leave the sorting for my sister, so she could find her reason to cry. It seemed a waste on me.

I tried not to think of the last difficult days of Mom's life...sitting beside her, holding her hand, brushing the hair from her eyes...already missing her as she slept around the clock. I thought instead of her good days, the days we walked arm and arm around her garden. She lived a good long life. People frequently remind me of that now, since her passing.

I was caring for my sister's plants while she's gone, and one evening, I hoisted a gallon jug of water over head to water one of her many hanging baskets on the back porch. I struggled to see what I was doing and to get the water on the plant and not myself. The water gushed from the pitcher over my head, missing me, but inadvertently washing three baby Wrens out of their nest! Two chirping feather balls spilled onto the deck and the third fell over the side onto the ground. I peered over the side as the birds wings fluttered wildly as it settled onto the grass three feet below.

I was not only startled but worried about their condition and future safety. They seemed *almost* ready to fly...but I felt certain they could not get back to the nest. I tried to pick one up to return it to its nest, but it flitted away refusing capture. The two on the deck eventually managed to get to a nearby tree, but the one on the grass didn't seem to have any intention of moving. Momma wren shouted at me from a nearby tree. I decided to wait a bit and see what the third one would do.

Later, Maggie and I went back outside to see if the wren had found safety and to turn off the garden sprinkler. In a blink of an eye I realized Maggie had scooped up the baby bird that unbeknownst to me still lay in the grass. I tried to grab her collar to save the fledgling but Maggie was not about to relinquish her treasure and ran gleefully away.

I was angry and upset...at myself and at Maggie. I wanted to slam a door, but I didn't. Instead, I went back in the house and left Maggie to her dog-ness, chastising myself for not thinking before I watered and then not thinking again before I let Maggie back outside.

She eventually came back in the house and plunked down on the floor beside me as I lay on the couch watching television. I scowled at her and she whined at me...a soft, plaintiff whine that I could not decipher.

When you continued to whine, even after I had quit scowling, I studied her to see if I could decipher what was bothering her. Her mouth looked out of whack somehow...puffy on one side or something...I suggested my husband take a look inside...in case she had a tiny bird leg caught in her throat or between her teeth. He found nothing.

Maggie continued to whine. I pulled myself up off the couch and got her a bone. Perhaps I had hurt her feelings when I had shouted at her to drop the bird, though I doubted she remembered or cared. Anyway, it was worth a try and my way of easing my conscience.

She opened her mouth to take the bone and as she did out popped the baby bird! Still completely in one piece! She took the bone. I took the bird, stunned and saddened by such an indifferent exchange.

My husband disposed of the sad little bird and I turned off the TV. I sat back down on the couch; Maggie now relaxed and curled up beside me. I had so many notes left to write to my mother's friends to inform them of her passing. So many people cared about Mom after ninety seven years on earth. I had been remiss in not writing sooner. As I wrote, I chose my words carefully, trying to soften the blow. I didn't cry or feel sad.

Before bed, Scott and I took Maggie for her nightly stroll. My sister's house sits on the side of a small mountain and the road in front of it is quite steep. I am convinced it is why she is so thin! She climbs it twice a day with Maggie. That night, as we climbed the hill, panting and huffing, we heard thunder rumbling in the distance. We quickened our pace as much as we could without passing out.

As we turned to head back home, the view of the twinkling city spread out below was breathtaking. Lightning flashed in the sky to the north to the north. It was off in the distance so we took our time enjoying the beauty and majesty of God's fireworks. The sky lit up purple and yellow, sometimes laced with spidery streaks. Between flashes it was pitch black. There were no street lights and the moon was behind a cloud. We carried a flashlight but left if off so we could enjoy the view.

As I walked down the steep slope, my eyes glued to the sky and Maggie as my only guide, I managed to step off of the edge of the road. My ankle rolled and I fell, face first down the forty five degree angle of the hill. It was an odd sensation; first my knee touched the pavement, then my shoulder and lastly my chin as I pitched forward and sideways.

I was stunned. My thoughts tossed about trying to figure out what had happened. Once I realized I had fallen I began to assess my condition in a detached, cerebral sort of way. Various parts of my body began to sting and I tried to bring my thoughts into focus. I was having difficulty determining the exact location of my various body parts and the degree of my injuries.

Scott dropped to the ground beside me, taking Maggie's leash from my stinging hand and wrestling with the flashlight to turn it on.

"Are you alright?" I heard him say. He sounded more frantic than I felt.

I couldn't respond still trying to find my center of gravity...physically and emotionally. The slope of the land forced me to work against it and my whole being felt out of kilter.

At last, I was mostly righted and he took my arm as Maggie licked my face. Seated, but now upright, I lay back on the ground exhausted from the struggle. Scott brushed the hair from my face, clearly frustrated by my lack of verbal response to his inquires, but after twenty five years of marriage he has become quite adept at handling me and just kept talking softly to me until I found my voice.

At last I managed to choke out a few words, but just as I began to find the words to tell him I thought I would live, my throat constricted and a flood of tears erupted. Something suddenly broke inside of me. Overcome with wracking sobs, deep, wrenching, waves of emotion washed over me. My husband, now sitting beside me on the side of the road, in the dark, Maggie at his side, wrapped his arms around me and held me tightly. He rocked me gently, whispering words of solace in my ear. My grief had found its way to the surface.

When the worst had passed, he helped me to my feet and we hobbled back to the house, arm in arm...the poor man working overtime to hold me up, shine the flashlight ahead of us and manage Maggie simultaneously.

I think I cried for hours...overcome by grief, loss, and physical and emotional exhaustion...difficult days spent with my mom in the end...lost youth, lost innocence...lost opportunity...lost words...lost love...the deepest sadness... ...the hardest goodbye... the loss of my mother.

My friend was right. I had not lost the ability to feel. I was just waiting for the right opportunity.

HOME IS WHERE THE HEART IS

Last weekend my husband and I drove from North Carolina to Vermont to bury my mother. It has been a long and winding road leading up to this journey. We left North Carolina in the morning and drove all day through Virginia, Delaware and New Jersey, stopping for the night in Suffern New York, our old home town. As we traveled I felt tugs on my heart strings as memories of our years lived in Virginia, New Jersey and New York flooded my already emotion laden soul. I spent four years in New Jersey going to school, two in Virginia caring for a two year old and having my second child.

New York...it is my home...it is where I feel most like myself. I've lived in the south over twenty years and yet I still come alive when I settle into a booth in a New York diner and look around at the diversity that surrounds me, the spectacular selection of food and the lay of the landscape outside the window of the restaurant. We are surrounded by people who are animated and friendly and fully engaged in their lives. It is after nine p.m. and things are still buzzing, a noticeable contrast to the quiet, and sluggishness of the south. We are out of rhythm with each other, the south and I.

After ordering omelets and bagels my husband asks me, "Do I look like I fit here?" I had to laugh. He is the quintessential New Yorker and belongs there more than I do. He doesn't fit in the south either.

The next morning we drive past our old houses, our high school and the church parking lot where we first made out when we were nineteen. I kept asking myself if it was nostalgia or something more. I still don't know. I just know I love it there. I love the feel of the air, the look of the sky, and the energy.

The next day we pulled ourselves away and head north to Vermont. My feeling memories carried me along. How many times had I traveled the New York Thruway? We recounted all of our shared experiences -- cars breaking down, snow storms, altercations at the toll booth (not ours, travelers)...then the green mountains of Vermont where I spent three years and many weekends visiting my brother, going to college, and skiing. It's not home like New York but it's a wonderful place that has a piece of my soul.

It's quiet, simple and beautiful, and I am glad my parents have chosen to be laid to rest there, beneath a tree, in a small, unsophisticated cemetery that dates back to the 1700's. My nephew, my brother's son who died at two, is there beside them.

Someday I will find my way home too.

DEAD HEAD

I'm blocked. My brain has come unglued. It's a disconcerting feeling that I blame on age whether it belongs there or not. I have never been wordless...in my head at least. Could be the onset of dementia but I hope not. I'm too young and I haven't realized my dreams.

I was the quiet, shy type as a young person. Actually, I was terrified of people. That seemed to vanish somewhere along the way, the terrified of people part, but I'm still quiet, outwardly. Words, however, swirl around in my head endlessly looking for a place to land. I've written so many letters, stories, novels in my head...if they were on paper I'd be rich...well, maybe not...but at least they'd be out there and not locked up in the dark recesses of my mind.

Right now, my brain is in neutral. I'm hoping it won't last forever. I haven't yet said my piece, though I dare say I don't know what that is. Rather than being terrified that I'll never get the chance, I spend my time thinking about what could be wrong with me. Maybe my dead head is something else. Lack of exercise. Too much sugar. Grief. Whatever it is, it is thoroughly annoying. How am I supposed to write and communicate if my brain is empty?

My time is running short. How I hate feeling that way. I want to feel that the future is endless the way I did when I was young. I don't want to keep remembering how old I am and how much time I've wasted. The worst thing about it all is that I have finally realized what it is I want to do and to start living only to find my brain has gone numb. Could I have lost my chance? That would be the worst.

Maybe I'll go for a walk.

MOVING ON IS NEVER EASY

Moving on is not an easy thing to do. We get used to the things we use to define us. They seem to become woven into the fabric of our being even when they are not who we really are.

Childhood experiences and memories often pop up out of nowhere; a smell, a sound, an expression on someone's face. Old hurts that we thought were well buried can rush to the surface given the right combination of events.

It's hard to turn our back on those things we thought we had let go of years earlier when they manage to wiggle their way back into our lives and consciousness.

It would be so much easier if we could just erase those thoughts and feelings we no longer need by pressing delete and launching them into the recycling bin.

THE GIFT THAT KEEPS ON GIVING

There comes a time in each woman's life when we look at our best efforts and see only the failure. We started with a dream or a mission or a purpose. We put ourselves behind it, believing without a doubt that we were on the right path. The path takes us on a marvelous journey to an ideal place. We devote days *or* weeks, months or years to our vision only to wake up one morning and realize our dream has *failed* or *vanished.*

What then? What do we do when we find ourselves curled up in a ball in the corner wanting to hide, the pain too great to even acknowledge? We ask ourselves over and over, what went wrong? What did I do wrong? What could I have done differently? And why, oh why, did it turn out this way? We want to curse the world, or the person who demolished our dreams...perhaps it is ourselves we wish to demolish...blaming ourselves for the failure, for our inability to see the future when we made our commitments. We all know that seeing the future is a gift given only to a few, if any. And yet, we expect it of ourselves.

Perhaps we are asking the wrong questions as we try to break through the confusion and the pain. Blaming others is futile even if it is a survival instinct. Blaming ourselves is equally as disastrous. The real question is what can I learn from this? What can I take forward with me into the rest of my life? What does this experience tell me about who and what I am -- the good *and* the bad? These are the questions of growth and survival.

Life is a learning experience and sometimes we have to learn the same thing over and over until it takes. As painful as that may be, we eventually do learn and then we have a gift to pass along to others. It is a gift that every woman has to give as she ages. Previous generations looked upon it with reverence and respect -- it is the gift of wisdom. It is the most we can hope to gain from our life's difficulties, but it is a gift that keeps on giving.

I KEEP SPILLING MY COFFEE!

Am I the *only* one who has this problem? The fact that I spill my coffee at least once a day is adding insult to injury when it comes to my view of my own mental stability and sense of self control. I fear I am not aging gracefully!

I used to think of myself as a person of style and sophistication. Not that I believed I was but because I desperately wanted to be. Some old boyfriend told me years ago that I had "class". I think it was the best compliment I ever received before or since. I always wanted to have "class" ... of some sort! No doubt it was just his method of getting a little action, but I didn't care. I took the compliment and ran!

I digress...coffee spilling...it's become an affliction! I drink coffee, or rather carry it around with me, all day long, reheating and sipping, reheating and sipping. That could be part of the problem.

I don't have a clue how much I actually drink. Like I said, I spill most of it...and I add more and more fat free half and half as the day goes on. Late morning I switch to flavored cream as the bitter taste of 4 hour old coffee gets the best of me.

My inability to keep coffee in a cup has given our off-white carpets a new look: lovely caramel colored spots in random locations perfectly suited to the whimsy of a modern art lover. I also find coffee spatters on the walls in the strangest places, managing to spill it without even being aware that I am doing so. It's worse than that.

I have a couple of wide mouth mugs that should be banned from use by people like me. I picked them up at TJ Maxx a few months ago. I'm addicted to pretty little mugs, particularly bone china. They chip and break just as I'm getting attached to them, so I stock up whenever I have a chance. I have a favorite at all times...I have mood mugs too...certain time of day mugs...tea mugs...soup mugs...I-will- never-use-that-mug mugs.

My preferred mug at the moment is a delicate, small bone china piece with a very even, steady pattern of tiny dark pink roses. It's the perfect size for my morning coffee and stays close at my side until after lunch and when I'm done with it and it goes in the dishwasher to be sparkling clean and ready for me the next morning. I prefer a heftier mug as the day goes on. Something more solid and substantial, like the beautiful royal blue pottery mug I purchased in a shop in North Carolina's famed pottery town of Seagrove.

All the beautiful mugs in the world do not keep me from setting my coffee cup unconsciously on the edge of a book, sending it head over tea kettle onto the floor, ruining not only the carpet and the walls, but my new Oprah magazine -- which I still will not confess to buying...even to myself.

I've become totally unconscious most of the time of late. I drop my makeup into the toilet of our tiny bathroom almost daily. It irritates me to my toes, much the way spilling my coffee does. I get so tired of scooping my mascara out of the cold (I tell myself clean) water when I *could* have put the lid down or better yet paid attention to what I was doing when I picked the thing up in the first place!

Today, I set my coffee on the end table next to the chair where I was sitting and working on my laptop. Of course I was not paying attention. I was trying to think about what I was going to say next in the piece that I was writing. So naturally, Murphy's Law being what it is, I set the cup just not quite squarely on the edge of the table but ever so slightly off the edge.

I haven't bothered to get out the carpet cleaner...I'm tired of all the wasted time and energy it takes to keep up with myself. I did the best to soak it up with a washcloth from the stack of washcloths my despairing husband purchased for just such occasions. The lovely white things are now tan. I told him white was not the best choice. He is ever hopeful of getting me on the straight and narrow.

My fear is that I am getting "mad cow disease" like my beloved friend, Denny Craine, who sadly will no longer be entering my living room on Monday nights. Why don't the networks let us have our good, decent dramas? My brain is befuddled...just like Denny's...and I'm denying it, much as he did. If only there was a pill or a computer program to help me figure out where I've gone amuck....

It would be so lovely to keep my coffee in the cup and my makeup in my hand and to be able to put a stream of coherent thoughts together when I speak. I really don't want to go out this way....

FRIDAYS

Here it is Friday again. On Monday I think, "wow, Friday seems like forever away" and then it arrives as if no time has passed. At least that's the way it seems these days.

I remember how Friday felt to me when I was young. The excitement percolated throughout the day--the anticipation of time off from school, fun and friends. In high school and college I felt that something exciting *had* to happen on Friday nights. The day was electric with expectation. *If* it was going to happen *that's* when it would happen.

On Friday night we shucked responsibility and went out and had fun! I'd got to basketball games or to movies with friends or out on a date with my guy of the hour. If I didn't have a guy, I'd make sure my path crossed with a guy I had my eye on. It was magical and fraught with teenage angst and enthusiasm.

Somewhere along the way the magic went out of Fridays. They have become a day like any other day. Life seems a kind of a monotone and when excitement does come, it doesn't come on a predictable schedule like it used to. It's random. I can't decide whether it is a function of age and, God help me, maturity...or something else entirely or a lack of joi de vivre.

A CHURCH PEW

The world is all a dither. The holidays are just around the corner. As I sit quietly writing, I can almost hear the clatter in the stores and the excited shrieks of the children who think they can't possibly wait another minute for Christmas to arrive.

My children have outgrown their childhood exuberance for the holidays. My husband is hard at work trying to make ends meet. I feel adrift. I don't have the energy or inclination to make myself get "up" for an occasion I've come to dread. I miss my mother more as the holiday nears and memories of recent shared Christmases swirl in my head.

Christmas has come to mean forced excitement, stress and spending too much money on presents that people don't need or want and too much time with family members we already see too often. Gone are the meaningful parts of the season. We quit going to church when the politics became more upsetting than the good we thought we could do.

As a small child, I remember lying in a church pew on Christmas Eve, my head on my mother's lap, eyes closed, listening to the priestly drone, as I was lulled to sleep by the familiar words of the Eucharist and the scent of burning candles. It was way past my bedtime, but going to the Christmas Eve service at our beautiful, old Episcopal

Church was a tradition and I was always invited. For one special night a year I was included in the adult world. I loved being in the dark, comforting, mystical church sanctuary....secure and safe...cradled in God's arms...and in my mother's.

A church pew, especially an Episcopal Church pew, is my safe place. As a child it was the one place where it was okay to be quiet. I liked being quiet. I liked immersing myself in something bigger than myself, to rest in a place that placed no demands on me. I could be myself. I could allow the fullness of my heart and the depth of my belief soar to the rafters and not have to explain the meaning to anyone. I could allow stillness to fill my heart and not have to speak.

I gave up my church pew--for a season. I thought I had found a different kind of safe place and yet I haven't. Secularism abounds, growing stronger and more prevalent each day. Maybe this Christmas it's time to find a new church pew -- a new safe place -- and step back into the arms of God.

FINDING PURPOSE

As I spend a few quiet days between holidays reflecting, I am once again reminded that life has more meaning when we have a purpose. I am more at peace with myself, and my life, when I am committed to something greater than myself; when I believe my actions and efforts are for someone or something other than my own gratification. I am somehow buoyed.

During the twenty some years I raised my children my focus was on their well being. My sole purpose in life was to help them grow and develop into happy, productive people. My commitment to this higher purpose made it easier for me to cope with the difficulties I encountered.

This became crystal clear to me when I decided to take my youngest son out of school in fifth grade and homeschool him. Even though it was one of the hardest things I ever did I believed right down to my tippy toes it was the right thing to do...for him. It made the sacrifices easier.

It's time to find a new purpose.

DOOM AND GLOOM

"Doom and gloom" is my husband's new nickname for me. He's shortened it to "D&G". It's winter. It's cloudy. It's rainy. And it's my time of year to slip deep into my melancholic nature. I say I have SAD. People seem to understand that concept. Yes, I'm very sad, always have been. Why? This year it's because I lost my Mom, but I can always think of a reason. Goodbyes are so hard and I've had too many. Depression can be relentless.

BUT! Even though I'm a glass half empty kind-a-person, my husband is the "glass-that-is-half-empty-is-actually-full-and-overflowing" kind. His incessant optimism can be downright infuriating! Can't he see the world is crashing in around us?? Get real!

I do thank God every day for him; for his humor, his love, his support, his encouragement, his willingness to call me on my shortcomings, his ability to grow and change, *and* his nicknames. He's my strength, my rock and the thorn in my flesh. I love him to pieces. He's the only reason I still believe in God. He was, after all, a direct answer to prayer and you better believe I cling to that when life seems hopeless as it does too much of the time.

And God! If we don't get some sunshine down here in the sunny south pretty darn soon I may have to install a refrigerator in my hiding place under the dining room table.

MY BIG YELLOW SUN

When I was a kid, and living in the spectacular state of Maine, I was too young to know it was the freezing cold backwoods of hell for some - my mother for one. It was home to me and I loved it. Sucking on icicles and building snow forts in winter...catching polliwogs and climbing on rocks in the summer...it was pure heaven for a kid like me. I have always loved the outdoors. I would live there if I could and if society hadn't taught me otherwise.

Things were rocky for me when I was a kid. I had health issues, school was pure drudgery, I was painfully shy, and the youngest of five kids. I didn't feel sorry for myself even in my sadness -- like most children I didn't really know life could be any different. As kids will do, I developed my own ways of coping. In addition to writing poetry, one of the things I did to cheer myself up was drawing a picture of a big yellow sun.

I'd scrounge around for the biggest piece of the whitest paper I could find and the best yellow crayon I had in my crayon box. The, I would fill that piece of paper with sun...radiant, glorious yellow sun! I always felt better when I was done. I'd hang it on my wall and feel the warmth shine down on me for the rest of the day.

Kids are amazingly resilient creatures. We would all benefit from looking back into our childhoods and relocating that creative, resilient being that still lives buried within us. That is where we will find the remnants of our authentic selves and the strength and wisdom to face life's challenges.

I knew the face of God then. I felt His presence in my day to day life; during those moments when I sat in the hollow of an enormous tree, soaking up the smells and sounds of its humming life force; when I was mesmerized by the enormous icicle that grew larger every day on the corner of our little house eventually reaching the ground; or when I was tantalized by the ragged flow of maple syrup from the tree in our back yard as we tapped it and gathered it in buckets; or when I was safely ensconced in the warm, safe pew of our church on Sunday morning, where the echo and aroma of reverence seeped into my soul; I knew God was there...with me...then.

A MOTHER'S LOVE

Today is my mother's birthday. She would have been ninety eight. It's been seven months since she left the earthly confines of her body to be with my father. I miss her every day -- some days more than others. She was a good woman, but more importantly, she was my mother.

Born in 1911, her life was very different from mine. Her father, a frustrated entrepreneur traveled from job to job, sometimes leaving she and her mother behind and at other times uprooting them once again so they could stay together. They often went without and because of the constant upheaval my mother barely attended elementary school.

In spite of her hit or miss schooling as a child, she was able to complete a college degree in a little over three years. She lived when life was calm and simple - no cars, no planes, no TV - at a time when the earth was quiet. She saw amazing advancements in aviation and automobiles, highway development and television. She took in each and every change that took place over her life time, embracing it with enthusiasm.

She was a strong woman who led with her weak side - much the way so many women of her generation learned to do. She was one of the most giving women I have ever known. She took in strays - people, animals, children in need of a home, young adults in need of an education or money, women in need of friendship. She was never a committee leader or a career woman...she was a caretaker of the downtrodden. If she saw a need, she filled it in the best she knew how -- even if it was simply a kind word or a batch of cookies.

My mother did not win any worldly prizes. She did not gain recognition for all that she did. Her husband and children took her for granted. She almost never asked for anything for herself. Needless to say she was worn thin much of the time and yet she soldiered on giving away as much of her time and energy as she could until she reached ninety seven when her well ran dry.

When her mind refused to work and she no longer felt useful, she struggled to find meaning when it became too difficult to give to others. She slipped away, even as I believe her body could have lived to be 100. Her purpose was gone.

I miss her, but I hold her close to my heart. I know she is with me and loves me still. As each day passes, the difficult, unsettling memories fade a little more. In their stead, a precious gem that was her uncomplicated love for me begins to form. I hold it tightly, reverently, lovingly as close to my heart as I am able. The pain of loss slips away and in its place is the knowledge that she embodied the essence and purity of a mother's love. She gave it freely to all who needed it.

Happy Birthday, Mom. I love you. Thank you for loving me.

THE FLEXIBLE ARE UNBROKEN

Women are gifted with the ability to be flexible. I know it doesn't always seem such a positive trait, and sometimes we do not believe we are, but women universally possess the uncommon ability to put others first, to see other's needs and adapt accordingly.

When our children are ill, we take off from work, rearrange our schedules and take them to the doctor. We are flexible. If someone calls in sick at work, we change our plans and take care of whatever needs to be done. We complete their "to do" list as well as our own. When an elderly parent calls us and tells us they are out of milk, we change our schedule so that we can stop by the store and then their house and deliver what they need. We use the money we saved for a camera for ourselves for our husband's emergency dental work. Women are givers and as such are also inordinately flexible.

It is a good trait, one that can and should be celebrated by women. Too often we diminish and demean our feminine nature, chastising ourselves for not being more attentive to our own needs. While that is undoubtedly true, perhaps we should just pat one another on the back and applaud each other for being so giving, so flexible, and so wonderfully loving.

Maybe if we celebrated our gifts and acknowledged that the flexibility we have developed from caring for others may be the very thing that allows us to survive, to forgive, to embrace, and to live to love another day. If we filled our hearts with gratitude instead of guilt, we might not feel the desperate need for "me time" that we think we need. Every day is "me time". Every time we choose to be flexible and to love we are being the best that we can be. That is "me time" too.

Maybe the old saying that the flexible are preserved unbroken is absolutely true!

YOUR BEST DESTINY

Too often we allow the people in our lives to take a piece of our heart and twist it into knots. We allow them to convince us that we don't matter, that we are not important, that we are not in control, and that we are somehow less-than. We accept their version of who we are and even begin to see ourselves from their perspective instead of our own. When it happens it makes me want to curl up in a corner by myself or lash out in anger and hurt them in return.

The truth is, we get to choose how we respond when those we love (or those we don't) make their choice to be insensitive or overbearing. We can choose to engage them or we can choose to walk away. One step beyond that choice is the choice as to what we do with our feelings about what has happened. We can choose to let the hurt fester or we can let it go and get on with life. None of this is easy.

Our parents were taught that feelings should be ignored. Their approach was to "pull ourselves up by our boot straps" and get on with life. Our generation entered the era of "feelings" where they were elevated to the pinnacle of importance. We believed we had to *feel* our hurts or we would never heal. As a result, we tend to spend too much time massaging our problems and never letting go of them.

Science has begun to recognize that feelings follow thoughts. If we change our thoughts, we change our feelings. The proponents of positive thinking and positive affirmations will convince you of this very quickly.

I believe that is a combination of the two. We are not simply our thoughts *or* our feelings, we are more than that. We are creative creatures with an evolving, erupting, engaging creative force within us that ebbs and flows and moves us (or not) ever closer to our essential selves.

Most of our problems occur when we resist this process and try to control it. We inhibit our growth and work against our happiness. We fare better when we let off the controls and allow our spirits to soar.

When we face a situation that locks us down or clams us up, it behooves us to recognize it as a situation that is taking us away from who we were meant to be. Then we must let go, and turn toward the creative force that is within each of us. It will lead us to our proper destiny ~ one that is always waiting there for us.

Rather wasting time and energy on people who do not love you or treat you right, our energy is best focused on our creative path and where it is leading us. That is where we will find our answers.

WANDERING LIFE'S SHORES

I've been away...wandering the shores of my life's discontent. I wish I could say I had found something along the way, but I haven't. Not yet. No new insights or flashes of inspiration have woven their way into my tired psyche. Instead, the hum drum of everyday life, as it wheedles away at my resolve, wreaks havoc on my devotion to the truth.

There are times in life...too many of them to my way of thinking...when things seem not to be going anywhere, no matter how hard we try. Lying back and listening to the breeze of relentless thoughts as they filter through the debris of daily routine only serves to nudge loose a pertinent reflection that has been wedged between yesterday and tomorrow. There is not even enough of a spark worth blowing on.

I hold the slightest of hopes, that what appears to be dumb numbness, is the winds of change that will eventually break loose the boulders of resistance and allow a new beginning to emerge. In the meantime there is nothing more to do than wait.

RHYTHM OF FEAR

My heart has learned the rhythm of fear
The white hot arc that dances beneath
The numbing pain of loss

Laid bare by malevolent thoughts of hope
Pulsing to the surface out of a dulled awareness
As longing remains tucked neatly in empty silence

Long forgotten songs of security lay fallow
Now terrorized by darkness drumming,
Dancing, releasing a fresh target of despair

I call upon a hymn of gratitude to purge
And anoint a thankful heart
To find a song of joyous celebration

Only to fall flat
Disquieted and alone
In the rhythm of fear

RELIEF

The sky is darkening. The thick summer air pulses with restless energy. A mower hums unaware of the roll of thunder in the distance. Clouds boil over head, quickly moving in and shutting out the light. The dog paces, agitated; participating in the unease that permeates everything.

I think about turning on a light, but I am not anxious to break the spell that has been cast. It seems as if it's up to nature to do that. Soon....the thick drops of rain begin to spill. The wind whips sheets of water down the street as I listen, stilled by the intensity, and wait.

The rumbling sky grows louder, as if shouting at the rain to move along more quickly...insistent, driving. The glistening foliage weighted down from summer's constant growth, and now this... the heaviness not to be relieved by the rain, only intensified.

We are all awaiting relief.

MORNING GLORY

A chorus of happy faces stands proudly beaming
Bold in their momentary beauty, as the rich
Strong vine that thrust them thus lies hidden

The glory of the morning smiles radiantly at me
Their history beguiling a less than careful gardener,
Now watching with gratitude for their determination

Purple, pink and blue, trumpets of summer,
An early riser's gift, a hummingbird's delight
Joyous until mid-day's heat renders them silent

To sleep beneath their canopy of green and
Store up their treasure for another morn

AND SO IT IS JULY

It's hard to comprehend that in two days a year will have passed since my mother's death. It has passed so swiftly. It has been a year of disconnect - from myself, my life - something came unhinged the day she died. I'm still not sure if I can define it.

Even though I have lived my own life and felt quite separate from her for years, she defined who I was in some very essential way. Who I was meant to be was a vision she carried with her to the end, though what is was, was never clear to me. She knew me and yet she didn't know me. I knew her, and yet I didn't know her.

I cried regularly for a month or more after she died but I didn't cry because I missed her. I don't know why I cried really. And now, I don't miss her all that much. I loved her, but she had become a burden, her manipulations, her guilt, her inability to express love without strings attached expectations...a self-centered viewpoint.

Even in the end she could not ask for what she wanted. How then could she ever let me ask for what I wanted? As a result neither of us even know what we want?

My husband told me more than once in the past year, "You must say good-bye to your mother." The first time he said that I turned on my heels and walked away, throwing back a resounding "NO", in response, as a knot welled in my throat. Each time he made the statement my feelings diminished. I cared less. I still refuse to even go there...wherever "there" is.

I have not said goodbye. Nor do I intend to. Why should I? What is the point?

AGING WITH GRACE AND STYLE

It's not always easy to feel good about ourselves as we age; about our appearance, our accomplishments, and our future. It's an uncertain time for many of us. Every now and then I am reminded that it is possible to grab a bit of dignity here and there along the way.

I was on vacation last week, taking a much needed respite from the stress of the last year. My husband and I, swinging happily on an outdoor swing, were gazing at a perfect view of the ocean. The day was glorious, the ocean breeze refreshing. We reminisced about days gone by and I, for one, was feeling melancholy. People passed by as they made their way from pool to beach and back again, slogging and squeaking in their "Crocs" and flip flops. We wondered why we were the only ones who were content to sit and swing, and then we remembered. We are now "seniors" and that's what "seniors" do! It made me shudder but it didn't make me move.

As we people watched, I saw a woman about our age approach pushing an elderly woman in a wheelchair. The little woman in the chair reminded me for all the world of my mother. She was no doubt in her nineties; small, spry and alert, wrapped comfortably in her sweater and hat despite the eighty-five degree temperature. What captured my attention, apart from her resemblance to my mother, was the huge smile on her face. This elderly woman was taking in everything around her with the greatest of interest and enjoyment. She was not about to leave one ounce of pleasure undiscovered during her day at the beach, despite her confinement to a wheelchair and her advancing age. My mother was like her in this regard, embracing the world every day she lived.

I realized as I watched the woman role by that I had something to learn from her. Life is not so much about the big things, as the little things, and there is so much enjoyment to be unearthed in each and every one. She epitomized what aging with dignity and grace should really be all about.

This charming little woman was not letting her last days on earth slip through her fingers by feeling sorry for herself. She was taking life by the horns in whatever way she could, even if it was from the passenger's seat. Perhaps she could no longer hop, skip or jump with the children, or lie languidly in a bikini with the young women, or even push a wheelchair down a path, but she could take in the beauty that surrounded her and relish the play of the children in the ocean waves. She had chosen to enjoy what was still hers in this life and so can we.

THE AUTHOR

In 2005, Dorothy retired from the small home improvement business that she and her husband started over eighteen years ago, to devote more time to writing. Her two sons have stepped in to take the helm of the family business in her stead.

Dorothy enjoys writing on issues of aging, personal growth and spirituality, and dabbles in fiction and poetry. Her numerous articles and short stories appear widely in print and online.

Links to some of her recent articles can be found on her website:

www.dorothysander.com and www.AgingAbundantly.com.

If you enjoyed this book, you may enjoy subscribing to Dorothy's blog: http://agingabundantly.wordpress.com

HISTORY OF WOMEN ETCETERA!

The fifty plus woman of the 21st century is very different from the fifty plus woman of previous generations. Where once women were winding down from their child rearing days and preparing to settle into the role of grandmother, retirement, and old age, now the older woman, more often than not, is opening a whole new chapter in her life. She may still be actively involved in a career, starting a new one or struggling with decisions as to how to productively spend the remaining 20 or 30 plus years of her life. Today's 50 plus woman is still ready, willing and able to engage life fully.

Life expectancy has grown dramatically and so has the population of women over 50, now numbering 32 million. We are healthier, more energetic and face a longer, healthier future, but we face enormous challenges as well. Some of these challenges are new to our generation, such as concerns regarding job stagnation, ageism, and issues surrounding equal pay, long term health care, career changes and divorce. Others experienced by previous generations, are still equally challenging to women today, such as empty nest syndrome, menopause, health concerns and aging parents.

All of these challenges hit hard and furiously as we enter the fifth decade of our lives, and more often than ever before, women are facing them alone and unsupported. The nearby support of extended family has become a thing of the past as people rarely stay in one community long enough to develop long term, supportive relationships. Religious communities have become less relevant to the modern woman and thus we are not only left alone and unsupported but left to struggle with spiritual, moral and ethical concerns as well.

Women Etcetera! was founded by four such women who believed it was time to reach out and touch the lives of their peers wherever they could find them and offer support, guidance and a place to go for information, education and friendship. What began as a dream and a vision has fast become an exciting and viable real life option for women over 50 everywhere.

Women Etcetera! was founded to support, encourage and direct this fascinating and vibrant group of women through the many transitions they face and to help them see these transitions, not as difficulties and obstacles, but as opportunities and possibilities. Above all, Women Etcetera! offers a place of support, encouragement and friendship and an opportunity to face the years ahead with hope and enthusiasm, rather than despair and solitude. Women Etcetera! knows and believes that women everywhere are ready, willing and able to continue to evolve and grow and use their God given talents to better themselves and the world in which they live.

Visit the Women Etcetera! Website

www.womenetcetera.com

www.ingramcontent.com/pod-product-compliance
Lightning Source LLC
Chambersburg PA
CBHW060407290526
45791CB00002B/645